A New Global Human Order

Cheddi Jagan

Edited by Janet Jagan
Foreword by Clement J. Rohee

Harpy

First published in 1999 by Harpy
855 Maple Avenue, Milton, Ontario. L9T 3M3 Canada

Printed in Canada by Point One Graphics Inc.

Canadian Cataloguing in Publication Data

Jagan, Cheddi
    A new global human order

Includes index.
ISBN 0-9684059-1-6

1. Economic development. 2. Human rights.
3. Internationalism. 4. International cooperation. I. Jagan
Janet II. Title.

HN27.C54 1999   303.44   C99-900166-3

Dedication

To all those
who are struggling against poverty, for peace
and for a better world.

Acknowledgements

I would like to thank my daughter Nadira Jagan-Brancier, for insisting that this book be published and for seeing it through to completion. My gratitude to Clement Rohee for assisting us in deciding which of Cheddi's speeches and writings should be chosen to be included in this publicaion, and for his very informative foreword.

My thanks to Vesna Mayer for prepress work and to Krishna Persaud for his many hours of proofreading.

Janet Jagan

Contents

Foreword
Origin of the Vision - The Late President Jagan

It was just after noon one Friday early in the year of 1993 when I received a telephone call from the late President Jagan; *"Hi there!"* came the familiar greeting on the other side of the line; *"What's new?"* I recall briefing him on the more pressing issues which the Foreign Ministry was dealing with at the time. We then went on to discuss Bosnia. Dr. Jagan wanted a statement to be issued on the matter. The question at the time was what should be the Government of Guyana's position on the "Carrington Formula" as a solution to the problem and whether any reference of this "Formula" should be reflected in the statement. I cautioned against making reference to any particular formula but advised that the text of the proposed statement be cast in the context of UN Security Council resolutions and take into consideration our own national interests. Dr. Jagan agreed in principle, but he wanted to go farther. We discussed the matter in greater detail and eventually agreed to a formulation that met with his satisfaction. The statement was issued subsequently to the media.

Our conversation then shifted to problems of development. This was of major concern to him. Dr. Jagan drew my attention to the 1992 UNDP Human Development Report. With the nimbleness of his analytical mind he shared with me his thoughts on the work of the Commission on Global Governance and made a brief comparative analysis between the Human Development Report and the Commission's analysis. He told me he had just had a look at the book which contained the findings of the Commission entitled, *"Our Global Neighborhood."* In the course of our conversation, Dr. Jagan shared with me some of his reflections on an earlier conversation he had had with the late Mr. Mahbub Ul Haq, Special Adviser to the UNDP Administrator with responsibility for preparation of the UNDP's Human Development Reports.

Sometime in late 1993, President Cheddi Jagan drew my attention to a view that was beginning to emerge in the Commonwealth Secretariat in preparation for the Commonwealth Heads of Government Meeting which was scheduled to be held in Cyprus in October, 1993. The emerging view had to do with a discussion that had crystallized in a memorandum on: "*The Emergence of a New Global Humanitarian Order.*" By coincidence, the United Nations General Assembly in December 1992 had adopted a resolution entitled "*New International Humanitarian Order.*" Dr. Jagan was also aware of this.

At this point I was then invited to his office and we went over the actual publications we had discussed earlier over the phone. Dr. Jagan became very absorbed in the issues. And as usual, he was very lucid and methodical in the presentation of his approach.

In the course of our discussions, the question that was looming larger and larger in my mind was what concrete conclusion was all this leading to? Then, as if in anticipation of a question from me, Dr. Jagan announced that he wanted to put these ideas down on paper. The thrust of his written presentation would be to call for the establishment of a New Global Humanitarian Order. This was the harbinger to the call for a New Global Human Order.

Through the collaborative efforts of both the Office of the President and the Ministry of Foreign Affairs, it took about three weeks to bring all the relevant issues together in a coherent way, to identify the core issues and recommendations and to place them in proper perspective.

In effect, Dr. Jagan was preparing to fire the first salvo at the Commonwealth Heads of Government Meeting.

At that meeting Dr. Jagan spoke strongly in favor of the Commonwealth drawing up "a Consensus on Development" to supplement the United Nations Secretary-General's Agenda for Development and Agenda for Peace. Dr. Jagan stressed the urgent need to recognize and treat not only the symptoms of the crisis but also the root causes and to elaborate on a sustainable global strategy for development. That was October, 1993.

By May 1, 1994, the first publication containing Dr. Jagan's thoughts on a New Global Humanitarian Order was published in

7

pamphlet form and was sent to every Head of State and Government the world over. Some months later Dr. Jagan on his own initiative published his work in a booklet, in which he expanded on his original views. This booklet, entitled "*Pushing for a New Global Human Order,*" was produced primarily for distribution at the first Summit of the Americas held in Miami, United States of America in December, 1994. This booklet was also given wide circulation internationally.

At the 7th Inter-Sessional Meeting of Caricom Heads of Government held 29th February - 1st March, 1996, in Guyana, Dr. Jagan took the opportunity to introduce the concept to regional leaders with a view to gathering their support on the subject. The meeting ended expressing general support for the call. During that same meeting, Dr. Jagan asked me to meet with Ambassadors Rudy Insanally, Havelock Brewster and Rudy Collins who were all present at the meeting to discuss the concept with a view to further refining it. We came up with three main recommendations; first, prepare for the NGHO's formal introduction, in the UN system, by way of a resolution in the Third Committee. Second, that President Jagan use the World Social Summit and the 11th Summit of the Non-Aligned Movement, which were held in late 1995 in Denmark and Columbia respectively, to promote the concept.

The third but most significant recommendation was that the word "Humanitarian" should be replaced by "Human." Dr. Jagan was to be advised that the word "Humanitarian" was more in sync with an interventionist approach by the West in response to man-made and natural disasters in developing countries. We recognized that his focus was on Human Development as defined by the UNDP in its annual Human Development Reports, and logically the New Global Human Order was more appropriate to issues pertaining to Human Development.

But Dr. Jagan took the consultative process further. In a note written to me on October 28, 1996, it was clear that Dr. Jagan was still thinking of defining the concept even further.

In his note, this is what he had to say:

Dear Clement,

After notice Paper Motion on Endorsement of the Georgetown Declaration on a New Global Human Order (1996)

*is passed by National Assembly, send a copy of resolutions to all
Parliaments.*

*Should we change name (New Global Human Order) to
Global Partnership for Sustainable Human Development as
proposed in letters from Japanese Prime Minister and Iqbal
Haji?*

This should be discussed at State and PPP/Civic level.

Cheddi

The motion mentioned in Dr. Jagan's note was unanimously
adopted by Guyana's National Assembly in 1996, on the same
date in October. Copies were sent later to Parliaments around
the world.

It was in August 1996, however, with the convocation by
Dr. Jagan of an international conference in Guyana dedicated
specifically to discussing the call for a New Global Human
Order, that the concept was given a tremendous boost.

The Conference brought together intellectuals and
academics from both the developed and developing countries.
Locally, participants came from the labor movement, the
University of Guyana, religious organizations and political
parties. At its conclusion, the conference adopted the
Georgetown Declaration on the New Global Human Order.

It is apposite to note that the fundamental thesis on which
Dr. Jagan advanced his call was the question of
interdependence, particularly between the North and the South,
between the developed and developing countries but with
human development as the unifying factor between the two
camps. Dr. Jagan was bold enough to point out that the
availability of new financial resources was critical for human
development. His was the view that developing countries,
because of their huge foreign debt burden could not embark on
the road to prosperity and that handouts, and mendicancy were
not the solution, nor was aid with strings attached. What was
needed, he argued, was a totally new approach which would
address the debt question and find new and innovative ways of
mobilizing fresh resources to overcome under-development so
as to enable the developing countries, in partnership with the
developed countries, to play a more positive and meaningful
role in the global marketplace, currently characterized by rapid
globalization and trade liberalization.

Following Dr. Jagan's death in March, 1997, the PPP/Civic Administration (re-elected in December, 1997) reaffirmed its commitment to the call for a New Global Human Order. In this regard, several initiatives have been taken. Dr. Jagan's work has been translated into the French, Spanish and Portuguese languages, thus enabling a wider understanding of his views and proposals internationally. At the same time, Government of Guyana Diplomatic Missions in capitals around the world are being encouraged to establish "Circle of Friends" for the promotion of a New Global Human Order. The idea here is to establish and develop a global network of like-minded persons and organizations supportive of the call to establish a New Global Human Order. Much progress has been made thus far in pursuance of this goal.

But what is of great significance is the fact that within recent times many world leaders have been echoing, if not advocating, a similar line of argument which in essence coincides with Dr. Jagan's call for a New Global Human Order.

It is important to stress that the most popular of the elements inherent in the concept is the call for a tax on global speculative foreign exchange movements. It has been established that a tax of 0.05% on the value of each transaction can yield approximately US$150 billion annually. Noble Prize winner, economist James Tobin, had recommended such a measure as a means of mobilizing new financial resources for global development cooperation and human development.

Interestingly, with the emergence of the global financial crisis, many world leaders are now advocating, albeit in different ways, precisely what Dr. Jagan had proposed since the early 1990's.

This situation vindicates the visionary approach of Dr. Jagan. It has also demonstrated his ability, scientifically and correctly, to interpret global political and economic trends and to place his conclusions in a correct political framework.

Further, he went on to advance and to associate himself with bold and imaginative proposals aimed at facilitating human development based on North/South partnership.

This is the legacy of Cheddi Jagan.

Clement J. Rohee,
Minister of Foreign Affairs.

Introduction
A New Global Human Order

This book is intended to fill a void in a world situation of great confusion and convulsions.

After the Gulf War, President George Bush announced a New World Order, but within a short time, what emerged was a New World Disorder. And, as in the post-Depression period (1930s) and the pre-World War II period, all kinds of "saviours" are descending on the people with quack remedies - the fundamentalists, the Religious Right, the Far Right, the Ultra-nationalists, xenophobists and neo-fascists. Demagogues like Hitler and Mussolini glibly bandied national socialism (Nazism) and practiced intense nationalism linked to racism (the master race) in their quest for political power in the service of vested interests.

Today, in a period of intense crisis of modernized monopoly capitalism, the demagogues are once again rearing their ugly heads. They must not be allowed to succeed.

Our times call for clear thinking: to diagnose the ills of our globe, to ascertain the root cause of society's growing problems and to formulate what must be done - a set of guiding principles and a program of action.

Certain concepts of democracy, human rights, regional integration, free trade, sustainable development, among others - are being discussed. These need to be examined fully - form as well as content.

Democracy is a vital ingredient of development. It must be representative, consultative and participatory. The people, especially women, must be fully empowered. The goal of democracy must be, as the American Declaration of Independence stipulated: "*life, liberty and the pursuit of happiness.*"

Human rights must embrace civil and political, as well as economic, social and cultural rights. Human needs and human security must be the object of development.

The economic basis is inter-related and must interact with the political, ideological, institutional and cultural superstructure. Economic growth is necessary for the satisfaction of basic needs and human development, as much as

11

human development is necessary for economic growth. There is a nexus between poverty, hunger, famine, malnutrition, homelessness, illiteracy, disease, population explosion, environmental degradation, migration, narcotics production, usage and trafficking, and crime.

Human development and the protection of the environment are closely linked. There will be no protection of the environment if the boundaries of poverty continue to expand.

Change is necessary. The "trickle-down" process under monopoly capitalism is not working. Instead, the rich are getting richer at the expense of the poor, and the gap between the developed and developing countries is ever-widening.

However, change will not come about unless a coalition of the left, democratic and progressive forces - the working class and the progressive sections of the middle class (petit-bourgeoisie) and the patriotic section of the capitalist class (bourgeoisie) - exercise state power.

My memorandum to Jacques Delors, President of the European Union, my Paper to the UN Hearing on Development and my Appeal to Heads-of-Government and others make the case for urgent radical reforms for a New Global Human Order - an Order providing for genuine North/South and East/West partnership and cooperation based on interdependence for mutual benefits.

Cheddi Jagan

Appeal For A New Global Human Order

Letter Sent to World Leaders from President Cheddi Jagan, May 1, 1994

This post-Cold War period has stimulated our hopes that a new world order can be established on the basis of mutual respect, equal opportunity for all peoples, the consolidation of democracy and human development.

A renewed opportunity is now afforded to place the welfare of our peoples at the center of national and international efforts. Our peoples have the right not only to political freedom but also to the full development of their attributes. To this end we should strive again, as expressed in Article 1, paragraph 3 of the **Charter of the United Nations**: "*To achieve international cooperation in solving international problems of an economic, social, cultural or humanitarian character.*" Only then can sturdy and lasting foundations for international peace and security be established.

We must resolve to reverse the gap which has been developing between the richest and the poorest countries. The divisions between the rich and the poor in the industrialized societies in the North and in the developing and underprivileged societies in the South, as well as the distance in attainment between the North and the South have been widening considerably since the early 1980s.

In the North, the consequences of these disparities have been unemployment, homelessness, urban disorder, increase in crime especially among the youths, the rise of ultra-right movements, strident nationalism and fragmentation accompanied by racism and ethnic tensions.

In the South, the consequences of these divisions have been the increase in crime and disease, hopelessness, emigration, environmental degradation, and the illegal traffic and use of narcotic drugs.

Taken together, there is a situation of despair, alienation and indifference.

More alarming, however, is the incidence of increasing

13

poverty across the globe. Poverty atrophies the vigor and initiative of the individual and deprives the society of incalculable human resources at a critical time. Its elimination will enrich our community and release a harvest of energy and skills. If left unattended, the expansion of poverty, with hunger, will undermine the fabric and security of the democratic state.

In December 1992, the United Nations General Assembly adopted a resolution entitled "*New International Humanitarian Order*." That resolution urges Governments, as well as governmental and non-governmental organizations, to provide comments and expertise for the Secretary-General regarding the humanitarian order, and to develop international cooperation in the humanitarian field.

In October 1993, the Commonwealth Heads of Government at their meeting in Cyprus considered a memorandum on: *The Emergence of a New Global Humanitarian Order*. That memorandum comprised a set of principles to govern the behavior of states to underpin the new humanitarian order and to prevent conflicts. Accordingly, Commonwealth Heads agreed to establish a high-level inter-governmental group to examine specific ways in which the Commonwealth can make a contribution to the work of the international community.

With this in mind, I introduced in March 1994, at the Inter-Sessional Meeting of the Conference of Heads of Government of the Caribbean Community in St. Vincent and the Grenadines, an item: "*The Emergence of a Global Humanitarian Order*." Caricom Heads discussed the item and agreed to work together at the regional level and in concert with a Commonwealth high-level group to advance the concept globally.

At the same meeting in St. Vincent and the Grenadines, we also supported a proposal by Dr. Carlos Saul Menem, President of the Argentine Republic, to establish an International Volunteer Corps for the Fight Against Hunger. The main objectives of this Corps of Volunteers, as you are aware, are to eradicate hunger and eliminate extreme poverty. Earlier in November 1993, Dr. Menem had transmitted the proposal to the United National Secretary-General with the intention that the Corps will operate within the framework of the United Nations.

These several efforts acknowledge a concern for the expanse of hunger and poverty. All societies, nationalities and systems of government are prey to their debilitating effects.

However, individual states or societies cannot deal adequately with this problem. The evolving globalized system necessitates a global response.

As I stated in November 1993, a development strategy for the eradication of poverty must be global and positive, not the South against the North and the North against the South, but the North and South in interdependence, cooperation and partnership. It would be disastrous for humankind if the East/West conflict of the Cold War era were to be transformed into a North/South conflict.

Among other pertinent responses to the crisis is the **Human Development Report 1992** published for the United Nations Developmental Program. The Report calls for a new global compact on human development: in essence, an agreement to put people first in national policies and in international development cooperation. The UNDP Report lists a number of objectives to inform international effort.

These include institutional changes leading to:

(i) The establishment of global institutions to respond to the global dimension of the existing human society. Global governance today is weak and is dispersed over a number of institutions, many of which are the exclusive preserve of the industrialized and wealthy states that exert tremendous power and influence on international activity;

(ii) The United Nations system itself also has to play a more central role in global economic management and should have access to larger financial resources. Important global issues like debt, monetary stability and international resource transfers have not been dealt with extensively in the UN system;

(iii) The Bretton Woods Institutions - the International Monetary Fund and the World Bank - have moved away from their original mandate and need now to concentrate on human development, as distinct from the means of development, positing human beings at the center of their deliberations;

(iv) Democracy has been making promising gains in the nation states. This development is also imperative for the international institutions. Reforms are necessary within the

15

context of the evolving global system where the general welfare of the peoples of our globe is central. Thus, the UN should assume greater responsibility for the formulation of development policy;

(v) The IMF can then be adjusted to serve as a global central bank, its original *raison d'être*: to create a common currency, maintain price and exchange rate stability, channel global surpluses and deposits, rationalize access to credits, and provide the liquidity and credits which the poor countries need separately;

(vi) The World Bank would then return to its original mandate to mediate between the capital markets and the developing countries by assuming the role of an international investment trust, creating a new loan window - an Intermediate Assistance Facility - that would help countries to graduate from the concessional International Development Association terms but not yet sturdy enough to meet the tougher terms of the World Bank;

(vii) A new Official Development Assistance (ODA), which can channel to the poorest countries two-thirds of ODA, instead of the present one-quarter, is also a priority;

(viii) Additionally, a system of progressive income tax should be collected from the rich nations according to their income and development needs;

(ix) The UN Conference on the Environment and Development (UNCED) offers an opportunity for both rich and poor countries to accept sustainable human development as an achievable goal. UNCED also seeks to ensure that the poor countries have access to technology to promote human development in a sustainable way. In this regard, the Global Environment Facility is a valuable mechanism and we would need to expand its resource base, enlarge the participation of the developing countries, expand its mandate to cover national capacity building and the environmental priorities of developing countries: water; desertification, urban degradation and acid rain;

(x) A greater role for non-governmental organizations in the reformed institutions without diminishing the vital interests and representation of the poorer South;

(xi) Urgent action to utilize the gains at the end of Cold War confrontation by further reducing military expenditure which had reached a peak of US$838 billion in 1987. The UNDP Report proposed that all countries should agree to reduce military expenditures in the 1980s by at least 3% a year. This would yield by the year 2000 a "peace dividend" of US$1.5 trillion. This "peace dividend" will give the wealthy countries a chance to direct more resources to a social agenda and to assist poor countries through debt relief. A new debt bargain can be reached to halt the current debt related transfer of $50 billion a year from the developing countries to developed countries;

(xii) Providing for equitable international trade both in goods and services so as to accelerate global growth and allow a more equitable distribution of its benefits;

(xiii) Creating sufficient job opportunities to absorb the annual increase in the labor force and to contain immigration pressures. To this end, I had suggested increased employment through reducing the number of days or the number of hours worked per week without loss of pay; and reducing the pensionable age without loss of benefits.

(xiv) A Works Program for physical and social infrastructure similar to that of President F.D. Roosevelt's New Deal;

(xv) Tax and other incentives for more research and the use of science and technology to create jobs instead of eliminating them;

(xvi) Greater emphasis on increasing and improving basic services in health, education, housing and nutrition.

I have outlined some proposals for a fresh consideration; some countenance major institutional changes and sustained mutual understanding. I am assured that there exists the political goodwill to construct a new order where the primacy of human development is the guiding principle. Preparing a peaceful and orderly transition to the twenty-first century is compelling.

These proposals are not exhaustive; they are merely indicative of the challenging options available. I am convinced that with coordinated international effort, poverty and hunger can be eradicated in our lifetime. What is required is the international collaboration to define a framework for action buttressed by the resources from the "peace dividend."

To this noble end I seek your support.

Dr. Cheddi Jagan
President, Republic of Guyana
May 1, 1994

Memorandum on Caricom Intersessional Meeting - St. Vincent, March 11-12, 1994

Presented by President Cheddi Jagan

The exchange between Mr. Michel Camdessus and the Caricom leadership was very fruitful. He was able to inject some optimism in the context of a growing mood of frustration and hopelessness.

The situation in the Caribbean in terms of socio-economic decline in this period of global stagnation and recession is approximating that of the 1970's when there were general unrest and upheavals in several countries - Curacao, Trinidad and Tobago, Panama, Nicaragua, Dominica, Grenada, Suriname. Under the Reagan administration, the Caribbean Basin was described as a "Circle of Crisis," one of several in the world. The outcome was the Caribbean Basin Initiative (CBI) and the CARIBCAN. But after more than a decade, these initiatives have borne little fruit. Today, the Caricom's major exports - bananas, oil, sugar, bauxite - are facing an uncertain future. And tourism, its major "industry," is faced with growing problems - foreign-based cruise ships, competition from other tourist destinations, crime and drugs. Industrialization, already in decline, is threatened by mass-produced goods with modernized production methods - computers and robots - in the North, and cheap labor and huge internal markets in South-East Asia.

Sir Neville Nicholas, President of the Caribbean Development Bank (CDB) estimates one third of the population of the Commonwealth Caribbean is living in poverty. Recent surveys indicate the incidence of poverty at about 43 per cent in Guyana, 33 in Jamaica and 23 in St. Lucia. Sir Neville told a two-day regional consultation on poverty reduction that in the 1970s there had been *"a general improvement in living standards of the broad masses,"* due to *"rapid expansion in public expenditure on social services, such as health and education."* However, since the 1980s many countries had been unable to sustain this level of spending because of *"adverse external events, inadequate or negative growth, chronic balance of payments and debt service difficulties, [and]budget deficits.*"

The Caribbean, the US "fourth border" and "Achilles Heel," comprised mostly of small islands states, needs special consideration: a Development Fund and fair, not just free trade.

Guyana, with its abundance of natural resources, can play a role in Caribbean rehabilitation. Regrettably, the vision of Sir Arthur Lewis, Nobel Prize Laureate, for the Caribbean did not materialize. Against the background of mass upheavals ("riots") in the 1930s Depression period, he wrote, in his 1942 paper "*Industrialization of the West Indies*," that the way to higher living standards and political stability was to industrialize the region, modernize agriculture and settle the surplus population in British Honduras (Belize) and British Guiana (Guyana).

Sir Arthur's thesis needs to be re-examined. In this regard, Guyana can play a key role in its implementation not only for poverty alleviation and movement away from the production, use and export of narcotics and emigration, legal and illegal, but also for political stability so necessary for the inducement of private investment and the maintenance of democracy. Experience has demonstrated that countries, even with high economic growth rates but without equity and social justice, can pose a real danger to democracy.

To play its rightful role, to assume its responsibilities for the upliftment of the Commonwealth Caribbean peoples and to meet its legitimate debt obligations, Guyana must perforce have high economic growth rates. Devaluation, divestment and huge foreign investments, especially by the Omai Gold Mining Company and Barama Timbers Ltd., contributed to high GDP growth rates during the last two years of the previous administration (Omai and Barama did not, however, contribute significantly to state revenue and foreign exchange earnings) but did not lead to human development. In the 1991 UNDP Human Development Report, Guyana was cited for its relatively low Human Development Index (HDI of 0.539) and was ranked the lowest in the English-speaking Caribbean, especially when cognizance was taken of the low per capita Gross National Product (GNP) of US$250. Also Guyana had the lowest per capita income in the Western Hemisphere. In 1992 and 1993 the HDI was 0.539 and 0.541 respectively.

Consider our plight. My government is encouraging foreign investment, which is needed for maintaining a high economic growth rate to facilitate our debt payments. However, there are many obstacles to this process. For instance, in the forestry sector, there are a number of potential investors, whose involvement will contribute not only to the growth rate of the GDP, but also significantly to the National Treasury. Four potential investors can add at the very start approximately US$1.6 million in revenue. But we are being told by one aid donor that promised technical assistance to strengthen the supervisory and monitoring capacity of the Forestry Commission would be provided only if a freeze is put on new forestry concessions. And a strong campaign is being waged to stop these investors not only for environmental, but also for other considerations.

Incidentally, Guyana has set aside 900,000 acres of pristine rain forest for research in management and protection of the environment and biodiversity. For this gift to the world, the Guyanese people should have been rewarded with a cancellation of its debt in a debt-for-nature swap. Instead, they have to meet some of the costs for this Iwokrama project!

We need sustainable growth, but this will not be attained with the huge debt burden, which consumes nearly 80 per cent of our state revenues and about 60 per cent of foreign earnings. These huge payments deny us the possibility of having economic growth and human development, which are, symbiotically inter-related and inter-acting: economic growth is necessary for human development; human development is vital for economic growth.

With our huge debt payments, there are inadequate budgetary allocations for wages and salaries, other charges, counterpart funds, health, education and social assistance for the destitute. Our PPP/Civic Government has set the poverty line at about US$49 per month at the existing rate of G$135 = US$1, but is forced to pay a basic minimum wage of about US$32. The Guyana Public Service Union (GPSU) claims that US$148 monthly is required for the least consumption of essential goods and services for a family of five persons.

With poor salaries and wages, it is difficult to attract personnel to, and retain them in, the Public Service. This leads to administrative incapacity and failure to implement projects for which, for instance, IDB funding had been attained.

As a result of malnutrition and a poor health care delivery

system, Guyana has the highest incidence of child, infant and maternal mortality in the Caribbean.

Due to poor salaries and inadequate teaching facilities, books, etc., our education system is not geared for this Information and Technology age. About 5% - 8% of children, age 5 - 6 years, are not attending school. Dropouts from basic education at age 14 were 61% in 1991 and 62.5% in 1992. Our results at CXC examinations in Mathematics and English are the lowest in the Caribbean. There are too few graduates from high schools in natural sciences due to the lack of trained science teachers and laboratory equipment, leading to few entrants to the University of Guyana and consequently only about 15% of graduates are in natural sciences.

The Minister of Housing in his 39-page Housing Policy Paper estimates that 90 per cent of the 4,434 houses that have to be supplied annually up to the year 2000 will need to be cheap and below US$7,404. At present low rates of wages and salaries, 84 per cent of households will be unable to purchase the lowest cost unit, since only 25 per cent of household income should be spent on housing. High mortgage interest rates are an additional inhibiting factor. And even at lower interest rates, many will still not be able to afford housing: at a 5 per cent interest rate, about half of all households with an average of 4.36 persons will be excluded; at zero interest rate 15 per cent will be left out.

In view of the above facts, Guyana is in dire need of relief from its very excessive debt payments. These have created a vicious cycle: the prevention of production capacity which is needed for earning not only additional revenues but also additional foreign exchange to offset excessive demand which has caused the exchange rate to go up recently. The vicious cycle needs to be replaced by a virtuous cycle: debt payment relief in various forms - debt forgiveness or write-offs, grants, conversion of regular loans to concessional credits, debt buyback, long-term rescheduling - for Guyana to join the mainstream and play its role towards human development domestically, regionally and globally.

Dr. Terry McCoy, Head of the Institute of Latin American Studies at the University of Florida, wrote in 1989 that Guyana was a microcosm of what was happening in the region and the US Government had a responsibility to fight for free and fair elections not only in Panama, Nicaragua and Haiti, but also in Guyana. This was done. Now, to safeguard democracy in the context of global confrontation and insecurity (note recent developments in Mexico), it is enlightened self-interest to provide debt relief to Guyana. Generally, Third World debt, according to Fiona Goodlee, Assistant Editor of the British Medical Journal, "*holds back world economic recovery, increases the spread of disease, feeds the international traffic in drugs, damages the environment, and increases political instability and civil war, thus adding to the global refugee crisis.*"

A good guideline for debt relief to Guyana is the 1989 Cartagena Declaration stipulating that the debt/service ratio should not exceed 20 per cent. With our debt/service ratio nearly three times the average (23 per cent) for the least developed countries of the world, more appropriate is the position of the British opposition parties that debt payments be limited to a maximum of 10 per cent of a country's export revenue.

Guyana merits such consideration. It is setting an example of good governance - representative and participatory democracy; consensus building; economic growth with social justice and equality; firm steps towards the eradication of poverty, extravagance, corruption and discrimination.

We have been responsible for the restoration of confidence in government and the empowerment of the people, which are vital ingredients to social progress. Our human rights record has been praised by Freedom House in New York.

We are extending democracy by holding municipal and village elections which were last held and rigged in 1970. At the grass-roots level, we are rapidly mobilizing the people in our communities through broad-based Citizens Committees for self-help activities in infrastructure rehabilitation and community policing in the fight against crime and other anti-social activities.

The Government has set its face sternly against corruption and extravagance. Several prominent persons and companies have been brought before the Courts on corruption charges. An Integrity Commission is soon to be established. In 1993, by paring down expenditure in the Presidential Secretariat and the Ministry of Foreign Affairs (under the previous administration, the latter spent more money than allocations for health, education, fire service and sea defense), my Government was able to find additional money for the police to combat crime and to increase expenditure for social services from 8 per cent to 14 per cent.

We realize that income inequalities and discrimination can increase the likelihood of instability, which in turn tends to reduce private investment activity. The new Government has pledged to reverse the trend during the 1980-1990 decade under the PNC administration, when real wages fell over 50 per cent and the rich got richer at the expense of the poor. We propose to enact a Race Relations Law and to set up a Race Relations Commission to fight against all forms of discrimination in our multi-ethnic, multi-cultural society.

The PPP/Civic Government is prepared to work with the international financial institutions (MFI's) and the other aid donors to maintain a stable macro-economic environment to provide the necessary framework for private investment. Indeed, we have surpassed the targets set by the IMF/World Bank. We are committed to a market-driven economy, with the private sector as the engine of growth. Private investment is welcomed and all obstacles have been removed. We look forward to fruitful dialogue, through which we hope we can attain our common objective of sustainable economic growth and the eradication of poverty. We have a rich experience in and out of government. In the 1957-1964 period, the PPP Government had made great strides in socio-economic development, with a mixed, tri-sector economy - private, co-operative and state. Human development is not simply technical/financial; it must be based on the science of political economy, not dogma. The economic base is inter-linked and inter-acting with the political, institutional, ideological and cultural superstructure. For us, politics is an art, based on principles, programs and policies with a high ethical and moral content.

In this regard, John Page, in his article "*The East Asian Miracle: Building a Basis for Growth*" in the IMF quarterly **Finance and Development** (March 1994 p. 2), wrote:

Much of East Asia's dramatic growth is due to superior accumulation of physical and human capital. But these economies were also better able than most to allocate these resources to highly productive investments. They did this with combinations of policies, always including market-oriented "fundamentals," but sometimes relying on tailored government interventions.

The MFI's and the aid donors, I suggest, must agree with us on the macro-economic framework and targets. How these targets are to be achieved must be left to our judgement: we take a world view and have a deep understanding of the concrete realities of Guyana. Our sovereign right of decision-making must be respected: we welcome consultations, but in the final analysis, the Guyanese people must decide their own future.

For nearly three decades, with the exception of the 1975-1976 and 1983-1985 periods, Western political, economic and financial support for the previous PNC authoritarian administration led to bankruptcy and Guyana being declared by the IMF in 1985 ineligible for further credits. Shock therapy, price liberation, removal of price control and subsidies, and unification of the exchange rate led to a surge in inflation. And a steep devaluation, led to declination of living standards and a leap in debt payments, amounting to 110 per cent of revenues in 1992!

A genuine partnership, based on dialogue and co-operation, is now needed to rescue Guyana and our interdependent "borderless world" from the deep and on-going cyclical and structural socio-economic crisis. Debt relief for Guyana is imperative at this crucial time by increased contributions from the aid donors and earnings of the MFIs.

It is my hope that, with the assistance of President Carter, the MFIs, the aid donors and the United Nations, Guyana can point the way forward. Let me conclude with the pertinent observation of Indonesian President Suharto, Head of the Non-Aligned Movement, to the recent G-15 Meeting in New Delhi: *"There is widespread apprehension that if the current international transformations are not managed with care and wisdom, the erstwhile ideological and political conflicts between East and West might well be replaced by an equally pernicious North-South economic and development divide."*

Cheddi Jagan

World Hearings on Development

Paper for UN-sponsored World Hearings on Development, June 6-10, 1994, by Dr. Cheddi Jagan, President, Republic of Guyana.

The New World Economic Order, proposed in the mid-1970s, after the first "oil crisis," did not achieve its desired goals. The "war against poverty" in the United States and elsewhere was not won.

After the Gulf War, President George Bush declared a New World Order, but within a short period, order had given way to disorder. What is urgently needed is a New Global Human Order.

But declarations and resolutions are not enough. They must be implemented by concrete programs and actions. Regrettably, the UN Development Decades and the development strategies and models - Puerto Rican "industrialization-by-invitation," President John F. Kennedy's Alliance for Progress, President Lyndon Johnson's regional integration ("ideological frontiers" replacing "geographical frontiers"), ECLA's import substitution, President Richard Nixon's Equal Partnership, President Ronald Reagan's Caribbean Basin Initiative (CBI), President George Bush's Enterprise for the Americas - have not solved the basic problems of national and personal security, poverty and hunger. But these problems now pertain not only to the South, the developing countries, but also the industrial countries of the North and the East (the former Soviet Union and Eastern Europe).

The Agenda for Development must elaborate a new strategy for development, which must take into account theory/ideology and appropriate practice, based on historical experience, a scientific world view and a concrete analysis of regional and national specifics and peculiarities.

Economics is fundamental, but for real development, other equally important factors must be taken into consideration. The economic base inter-relates and interacts with the political, institutional, ideological and cultural superstructure.

Unlike the periods of post-World War I and post-Depression of the 1930s, today's world is driven by the "technological revolution," the "information revolution" and the so-called "information super-highway." In the earlier period of the downside of the cyclical crisis of capitalism in the Depression period of the 1930s, the magic Keynesian formula was "pump-priming" - physical, social and cultural infrastructural works by President F.D. Roosevelt, and radical reforms by his New Deal Governor of Puerto Rico, Rex Tugwell, who advocated the breakup of the huge plantations of around 10,000 acres by reinstituting the Foraker Act of 1900, which had restricted holdings to no more than 500 acres, and established six state-owned economic ventures. In Sweden's "middle-way," the unemployed received 100 per cent of their wages and salaries. And in Britain, under the Beveridge scheme, the welfare state was initiated.

Now, the socio-economic crisis is compounded; it is cyclical and structural. The situation is more complex. Keith A. Bezanson, President of the International Development Research Center (IDRC) says:

There are, I believe, six new or rapidly changing features that define the current context not just for "development" in the South but also for all aspirations for improving the human condition. They are: a dramatically changed political context: economic globalization; wholesale changes in the content and direction of international trade; the unprecedented pace of scientific and technological innovation, major global shifts in socio-cultural value systems; and environmental globalization.[1]

The production process is modernized through cybernetics and robotics - computers and robots - in order to cheapen the product so as to be more competitive and to capture a greater share of the global market. This leads, on the one hand, to intense trade competition, trade barriers and protectionism; and on the other, to greater unemployment - joblessness even with economic growth - and social inequality, with a widening gap between the rich and the poor and large numbers of workers becoming marginalized.[2]

This is due to the fact that the modernized capital-intensive production process requires finance capital for research and new technology for the means of production, thus necessitating a greater share of the product for capital.

With structural unemployment and chronic budget deficits in most of the OECD countries, the Keynesian model is not applicable, the welfare state is withering away and the social security safety nets are being eroded.

Structural unemployment has increased to 35 million in the OECD countries and 20 million in Europe alone. The globalized marketplace is shifting some jobs to the South, and "*that shift is making the discarded workers of the North poorer and very, very angry,*"[3] as was demonstrated particularly in France in recent times. And with more workers being put on the dole, there is little room for work for the graduates of colleges and universities. Bezanson estimates that by the year 2015, "*around 700 million new job seekers will be entering the labor market in one year alone. 700 million! That figure is staggering when we realize that less than 50 million will knock on the doors of the global labor market this year.*"[4] As regards Big Business, he notes:

"*Much deeper than the end of the Cold War and the breakdown of ideology is the supplanting of the nation-state itself by the new forces of transnational and supranational entities. The effects of these new forces cross all boundaries. They are fast rendering meaningless the intellectual basis for differentiation along a North-South axis. A more accurate reflection of what is happening between and with societies is increasingly to be found on an "included-excluded" axis... The investments of transnational and supranational entities are unlikely to be the kinds of investments that the poverty-riddled parts of the world require: basic infrastructure, health, education, and fundamental services for the integration of populations into their own economies and societies. Since the 18th century, these are the kinds of investments that have been made by the nation-state.*"[5]

Businessmen want a marginal role for the state. Their philosophy is less government in business and more business in government. On the one hand, they do not want government to interfere; everything must be left to free competition and market forces. On the other hand, they want the state to provide the unprofitable infrastructure facilities such as roads, sea defenses, drainage and irrigation, etc. This has led to debt payment and balance of payment problems, especially with very high earnings on foreign investments in the profitable agricultural, industrial and service sectors and the drain of super-profits overseas.

In Latin America and the Caribbean, there was a net annual outflow of $36 billion due to dividend, principal and interest payments in the 1981-85 period, which greatly contributed to the "lost decade" of the 1980s. In this regard, Chile's former President Salvador Allende and the President of the Supreme Court had proved that the subsidiaries of the foreign copper and nitrate mining companies had received profits on investments on an average around 70 per cent, compared with about 12 per cent by the parent companies at home. This led to his minority socialist/communist administration receiving, after commitment to respect fully all constitutional guarantees, full support in the National Assembly of the conservative and liberal parties for the nationalization of the mining companies; to the imposition by the Andean Pact countries (including Chile) of some restrictions on foreign capital; and a call for the United Nations to set up a Center for Transnational Corporations and to elaborate a Code of Conduct for them.[6] Earlier, one of the reasons for the military overthrow of Brazilian President Joao Goulart in 1964 was his attempt to limit the amount of profit going abroad to not more than 12 per cent.

Certain social scientists, in contrast, see a greater role for the state in development to attain social justice. They recognize that historically, capitalism, as a socio-economic system, was more efficient and productive than the feudal system which it replaced. However, the free competitive state developed in the monopoly stage with sharp practices. Thus the need, as in the USA, for anti-monopoly regulatory measures like the Sherman Anti-Trust Act.

The Socialist World System and Collapse

Czarist tyranny and oppression and feudal and capitalist exploitation led to revolutions in 1905 and 1917 in Russia, the first unsuccessful and the second successful.

After the October Socialist Revolution of 1917, there was a period of outside intervention to destroy the first workers' state. This led to the creation of a highly centralized state and "war communism."

Since the workers and the peasants, who made the revolution, did not have the technical, professional and administrative skills to manage the state, an intellectual-bureaucratic strata developed and eventually took on a life of its own. Consequently, the state was democratic in theory but in practice was more and more centralized and bureaucratic. This eventually adversely affected the economy, production and productivity.

In this new situation, Vladimir Lenin elaborated his "*New Economic Policy*" (NEP), which adumbrated the role of the private sector in the economy.

Joseph Stalin, who succeeded Lenin to the leadership of the Communist Party, embarked on a program of rapid collectivization. This continued during and after World War II and reinforced the highly centralized, bureaucratic state.

In Yugoslavia, Marshall Tito established a new state system with workers' self-management, which was different from the Stalin model. A Bulgarian leader once described the Yugoslav model as one with no central planning and the broadest democracy, with self-management and total independence of each state enterprise.

Mikhail Gorbachev in a critique of the Soviet model under his predecessors, Stalin and Brezhnev, pointed out that a bureaucratic/command type of government and a bureaucratic/command type of management were responsible for economic stagnation. He introduced the concepts of Perestroika (reforms) and Glasnost (openness). The struggle for power by the various factions of the political power-elite led to collapse.

Felix Rohatyn, senior partner of Lazard Freres and Company, commenting on the collapse, observes that competition today is essentially driven by economic, as opposed to military and ideological issues, as Western Europe, North America, Japan, China and South East Asia approach the turn of the century. He noted:

"*One result of this situation is the widely accepted conclusion that the colossal economic and political failure of communism was due to the perfection of a Reaganesque or Thatcherite version of Free market capitalism. This conclusion is dangerous for two reasons*:

First, it is not true. Communism collapsed mainly because of its internal inefficiencies and contradictions once modern communications and technology made it impossible to continue in isolation.

31

Second, because it leads to the easy and unproven assumption that pure market economies can deal with technologically-driven productivity growth, defense cutbacks, and foreign competition, and that they can simultaneously provide high levels of employment and continued improvement in the standard of living of a large majority of the population."[7]

Need for Change

In the present alarming situation, there is a nexus between unemployment, poverty, hunger, famine, disease, infant and maternal mortality, illiteracy, population growth, environmental degradation, narcotics, crime and migration. It is necessary not merely to treat the symptoms but to attack the roots of the problem.

To achieve change, there is need for a people-centered program and policies embracing:

- Democracy - political, economic/industrial and social-representative and participatory with people's empowerment at all levels;

- A balanced productive/infrastructure development of the economy and simultaneous emphasis on industry and agriculture;

- Economic growth with social justice and eco-justice;

- Meeting the basic needs of the people;

- Good governance with equity and respect for civil and political, as well as economic, social and cultural rights;

- A war against all forms of discrimination, political patronage, nepotism, bribery, corruption and extravagance;

- A social contract between the state, capital and labor, with an accompanying ideology of industrial peace: a strong trade union movement willing to discipline its members and the employers willing to discipline each other;

- Multi-culturalism: unity in diversity.

The Role of the State and Private Sector in Development

Equally important as a correct strategy, programs and policies for sustainable development, is the question of political power and who controls the state. If the social contract is to attain the objective of economic growth with equity, with social justice and eco-justice, then the balance of power must be in the hands of the working class in alliance with the revolutionary democrats (the progressive sections of the middle strata).

As regards the role of the public sector and the private sector, the UNDP Human Development Report 1991 is relevant: It noted:

"While private spending on human development is quite important in both developing and industrial countries, the public sector often plays a critical, complementary role, especially where incomes are low and basic human needs would otherwise remain unmet. But public action in support of human development can take several forms. It can be policy action aimed at activating private initiative. It can be the provision of public finance to subsidize privately run services. Or it can be public finance for publicly run programs. Whatever the approach or mix of strategies adopted, past development experience shows that markets alone cannot ensure good human development; and neither can overextended public sector spending, because it is not sustainable."

And about privatization, the UNDP Human Development report 1993 states:

"Privatization is no panacea, however. Hastily conceived or executed, it might achieve very little. Privatization should thus be seen not as an end, but as a means to higher levels of human development."

Human Rights in East and West

The United Nations has adopted two covenants on human rights - the Covenant on Civil and Political Rights and the Covenant on Economic, Social and Cultural Rights.

Generally, the West emphasizes civil and political rights, whilst economic, social and cultural rights were prioritized in the East.

In the fight for civil and political rights and democratization in the East, and the ensuing turmoil, economic, social and cultural gains were lost. Rohatyn says that there was a "*crushing let down. Inflation, corruption, insecurity and humiliation have replaced the political fear and relative economic security which characterized communist regimes.*"

Armed with the free vote, the people in Poland, Hungary and elsewhere are now casting their ballots for the ex-communists organized in democratic/left parties: they want not only to preserve their newly-won democratic freedoms but also in the present situation of high unemployment, rapid decline in living standards, crime and insecurity, to recover the gains they had made.

To attain peace and security, development is essential. Urgent action is required on the basis of a New Partnership and a global strategy based on democratization and radical reforms.

After the Cuban Revolution, President John F. Kennedy advocated monetary, fiscal, land and administrative reforms for Latin America and the Caribbean. In introducing his Alliance for Progress on March 13, 1961, he had pleaded for reforms:

"*Those who possess wealth and power in poor nations must accept their own responsibilities. They must lead the fight for those basic reforms which alone can preserve the fabric of their own societies. Those who made peaceful revolution impossible will make violent revolution inevitable.*"[8]

However, those reforms were not carried out by the Latin American oligarchy - the triarchy of power (the military, the upper clergy and the latifundistas) - with tragic consequences for the people.

Today, with "aid fatigue" and cuts in overseas assistance, a co-ordinated global effort is needed to mobilize the necessary funds for economic growth and human development. More than a decade ago, the Final Document of 1978 of the Special Conference on Disarmament pronounced: "*Mankind is confronted with a choice: we must halt the arms race and proceed to disarmament or face annihilation.*" With the end of the Cold War, nuclear annihilation has been averted. But today poverty and all its consequences are the gravest threat to national security, individual security and peace. In the 1987-94 period, military expenditure declined by 3 per cent a year, yielding a peace dividend of US$935 billion, which regrettably has not been used to finance the world's social agenda. During 1995-2000, with similar cuts by 3 per cent a year, US$460 billion would be raised for development.

Other funds can be raised, as suggested by the Human Development Report 1994, such as demilitarization funds, pollution taxes and taxing global foreign exchange movements. A tax of only 0.05 per cent on the value of each transaction could raise US$150 billion a year. (Nobel Prize winning economist James Tobin has suggested 0.5 per cent).

Under the auspices of the United Nations, these funds can be distributed to both the developed and developing countries for a social agenda - the alleviation of poverty and the development of human resources.

Debt relief and other forms of assistance can be provided to states like Guyana which are saddled with huge debt payments.

In the industrial countries, infrastructure work programs, such as those implemented by President F.D. Roosevelt's New Deal administration, can be put in place.

The work week can be reduced to 35 hours or 4 days per week and the pensionable age reduced by 5 years without loss of pay and benefits, respectively.

Tax and other incentives can be granted for the use of technology which will be job-creating.

The United Nations must become the center for economic growth and human development, for radical reforms towards the creation of a New Global Human Order.

Notes:

1   Keith A. Bezanson, Iwokrama Rain Forest Program: First Foundation Day Lecture, Georgetown, Guyana, June 5, 1994, p.5.

2   The Pope has been very critical of market forces for marginalizing various sections of the working people, and "unethical capitalism" for bribery and corruption in many states, particularly with defense contracts.

3   Keith A. Bezanson, op. cit., p.6

4   Ibid., p.3.

5   Keith Bezanson, op. cit., pp 5 and 6.

6   According to the UNDP Human Development Report 1994, page
     87: Transnational Corporations (TNCs) control more than 70% of
     world trade and dominate the production, distribution and sale of
     many goods from developing countries, especially in the cereal
     and tobacco markets. An estimated 25% of world trade is
     conducted as intrafirm trade within TNCs. This concentration of
     power can also be damaging. To some extent, transnationals have
     escaped regulation by national authorities, and the speed and ease
     with which they can restructure their assets, relocate production,
     transfer their assets, transfer technology and indulge in transfer
     pricing have become a matter of international concern. TNCs have
     also engaged in oligopolistic practices and shown insensitivity to
     environmental concerns (more than 50% of green house gases are
     thought to be generated by their operations).

     There is thus a strong case for some international supervision of
     TNCs. A useful starting point would be to complete the UN Code
     of Conduct for Transnationals, which after 20 years' work has not
     been negotiated. This could be followed by the creation within the
     UN of a World Anti-Monopoly Authority.

7   Felix Rohatyn, Interlocking Fates: The West and The Rest,
     Stabroek News, Georgetown, Guyana.

8   Quoted in Richard Hart's Memorandum to House of Commons
     Foreign Affairs Committee, with special reference to Jamaica and
     Grenada, on Security, Stability and Development in the Caribbean
     and Central America; London, March-April 1982, p. 17.

Guyana Parliament Supports Call for Global Strategy to Combat Poverty

Sixth Parliament of Guyana, First Session (1992-1994)
National Assembly Resolution No. 37

WHEREAS there is widespread concern over the increase of poverty and hunger and that during this post-Cold War era human development should be accorded the highest priority in national policies and in international development co-operation; and

WHEREAS in December 1992 the United Nations General Assembly, convinced that solving humanitarian problems required international co-operation and harmonization of international action, adopted a resolution entitled: "New International Humanitarian Order," urging Governments to provide comments and expertise to the Secretary-General regarding the humanitarian order and to develop international co-operation in the humanitarian field; and

WHEREAS the Commonwealth Heads of Government at their meeting in Cyprus in October 1993 considered the matter "The Emergence of a New Global Humanitarian Order" and agreed to establish a high-level intergovernmental group to examine specific ways in which the Commonwealth can contribute to the work of the international community; and

WHEREAS Guyana is a member of that Commonwealth high-level intergovernmental group; and

WHEREAS Guyana introduced an item on the matter at the Inter-Sessional Meeting of the Conference of Heads of Government of the Caribbean Community in St. Vincent and the Grenadines in March 1994 which agreed to work together at the regional level and in concert with the Commonwealth high-level group to advance the concept globally; and

WHEREAS the Conference of Heads at the said meeting in St. Vincent and the Grenadines supported a proposal by Dr. Carlos Saul Menem, President of the Argentine Republic, to establish an International Volunteer Corps for the Fight Against Hunger; and

WHEREAS the President of the Co-operative Republic of Guyana, Dr. Cheddi Jagan, has written to a number of Heads of State advancing proposals for a development strategy for the eradication of poverty, which took account of certain recommendations of the Human Development Program, and seeking the support of Heads of State for a global response to these global problems;

RESOLVED that this National Assembly support the call for a global strategy to combat poverty and hunger as a priority in the New Global Humanitarian Order.

Passed by the National Assembly on June 27, 1994.

Paper to the European Commission

**Paper presented to the European Commission
by President Cheddi Jagan, September 1994,
Georgetown, Guyana.**

The Caribbean region was described in the early 1980s by the Reagan administration as a "circle of crisis" among others in the world. This was after upheavals in many Caribbean Basin countries - Trinidad and Tobago, Curacao, Panama, Nicaragua, Dominica, Grenada, Suriname and elsewhere - following the "oil crisis" and recession in 1973-74, and in quick succession after 1977, a second oil shock, falling terms of trade and extremely high interest rates.

In early 1976, the former Commonwealth Secretary-General (later Deputy Secretary-General of UNCTAD and UN Assistant Secretary-General, and Vice-Chancellor of the University of the West Indies) Sir Shridath Ramphal told the Summit meeting of the Caribbean Economic Community that the region was faced with "unprecedented difficulties" including a 20 per cent inflation rate, the scandalous food importation bill of US$1,000 million, a worsening balance of payments problem, and the need for 150,000 jobs for full employment by 1980. And he also lamented the shortage of funds for the public sector and "startling increases" in consumption expenditure.

Today, nearly two decades later, after some trade concessions by the United States of America and Canada, numerous diagnoses by "12 wise men," 20-odd academics and technicians, the prestigious West Indian Commission as well as structural adjustment, the Caribbean region is again in a serious crisis situation. The food importation bill is now over US$2 billion. Less than 10 per cent of total trade is among the Caribbean Community countries. Unemployment has soared and the "unprecedented difficulties" have been exacerbated.

Need for Change

The continued inability of regional economies to provide sustained improvement in domestic living levels is posing major challenges for change. But generally, emphasis is put mainly on domestic changes. We are told to embark on structural adjustment programs, increased trade liberalization, deregulation, privatization/divestment, an improved climate for private investment and private business activity, higher expenditure for infrastructure, expanded human resource development activities to improve administrative capacity, and an expanded monitoring and regulatory capacity as private sector activities expand and become more complex.

Regrettably, the structural adjustment programs have proved to be mere palliatives, not a cure. Structural adjustment has come at a heavy cost. Generally, it has come with:

- drastic budgetary reduction in expenditures on social services and subsidies on essential goods, which necessitate massive retrenchment in the public sector and undermine the human condition, the enabling environment and the potential for future development;

- an undermining of food production and self-sufficiency, leading to undesirable environmental degradation, and with coca and marijuana substituting for food production;

- an erosion of the capacity of infant industries, thereby slowing industrialization;

- a credit squeeze, which leads to an overall contraction of the economy, declines in capacity utilization and an accentuated shortage of critical goods and services;

- a generalized devaluation, which leads to socially unsupportable increases in the price of critical goods and services, raises the cost of imported inputs, diverts scarce foreign exchange to speculative activities, and exacerbates capital flight and triggers general inflation;

- unsustainably high real interest rates, which become a disincentive to productive investments and shift the economy towards speculative and trading activities.

Massive poverty is hindering the path to sustainable human development. Because poverty is so widespread and social inequity is so extensive, we need structural adjustment with a human face - a philosophy of humanism and a humane social order. It is necessary to have a redistributive social policy to bring about the needed changes through a heavy investment in human resources. Economic adjustment must be combined with social adjustment; economic growth and human development are interlinked and interacting - economic growth is necessary for human development as much as human development is essential for economic growth.

We need a correct theoretical perception of events, not only of the development of productive forces, but also of the relations of production and their contradictions. Piecemeal management is not enough. Nor can everything be left to be regulated only by the market. Both the market and the state, as the World Bank has noted, have irreplaceable, complementary roles.

We need action and goal-directed structural change, based on the theory of history and the theory of society. A comprehensive strategy for the entire society is required, based on the systematically-elaborated, rational model for the establishment of reasonable social relations.

The two UN Covenants on Human Rights, emphasizing civil and political rights as well as economic, social and cultural rights must be our guiding stars. High levels of human development are generally achieved within the framework of high levels of human freedom.

We must elaborate a rational model of development, not simply for economic growth, but also for human development. We need growth with social justice and eco-justice. There will be no solution to environmental questions, for instance, if the boundaries of poverty continue to expand.

We have today within our grasp through the advancement and application of science and technology, the opportunity not only to halve the level of poverty world-wide by the end of this century, but also to guarantee a generally high material standard of living. But this would be possible only if a just system of allocation and distribution were put in place. One of the most pressing problems contributing to a vicious cycle of poverty is the huge debt burden. Since the early 1980s, the Latin American and Caribbean countries have honored their debt obligations at the cost of tremendous suffering of the masses of the people, yet, the debt continues to grow. According to the 1992 UNICEF publication **Children of the Americas**: "*Between 1981 and 1990 Latin America spent US$503 billion on foreign debt payments (US$313 billion in interest). At the same time, the region's consolidated external debt rose from US$297 billion in 1981 to US$428 billion in 1990. This mechanism whereby 'the more you pay the more you owe' is perverse and must be stopped.*"

The cost of the debt crisis has been extremely high: living standards at the end of the 1980s in many developing countries had fallen to the levels of the 1950s and 1960s. The Caribbean Community or Caricom countries are burdened with a huge foreign debt of over US$9 billion.

Guyana's foreign debt was US$2.1 billion at the end of 1991, perhaps the highest per capita in the world (US$2,785). The foreign debt/service ratio in 1992 was an absurd 68% of merchandise export income, and total budgetary payments in the same year were 96% of current revenue.

We cannot achieve the articulated, the well-linked and the enlightened modernization of production if the State is burdened with enormous debt and with inherited structures that have no room to make way for new activities. When the debt burden is great, there are no resources for acquiring the knowledge and the new ideas to manage the economy and to train workers for productive employment.

When our inherited production structures face new markets but cannot transform overnight to new opportunities, we need help. We in the Caribbean do not need lessons on the need to export. We have done nothing else for four centuries without developing. Much of our production has for centuries been associated with exports - sugar, oil, bauxite, rice, citrus and coffee. Some of these structures have become uncompetitive in part because absentee ownership did not regard shifting to new activities as an imperative. In the meantime, our leading local businessmen preferred to expand as shop-keepers. There was some change to import substitution, but only recently do we find concerted efforts to seek external markets for non-traditional exports.

There is a high institutional and systematic and even cultural cost to the transformation of the very old trading regimes. Guyana and, to a lesser extent, Jamaica, have the additional cost of the removal of excessive debt burdens. These are not costs that we ourselves can meet. When we turn to institutions like the Inter-American Development Bank, we are often told that apart from Guyana, Caricom countries have to borrow at interest rates which are close to market rates. If this continues, there will soon be no need for development banks since the conditions on which the countries can borrow approximate so closely to commercial terms. Almost all the economies in the Caribbean are growing too slowly to borrow at today's real rates of interest of 5% and 6%. May I remind you that at a meeting of ECLAC in Chile in 1961, I had referred to such interest rates as a contributor to the debt crisis which was then in the making.

In the case of Guyana, there is no scenario presented to us that indicates that our intractable debt burden, which circumscribes economic and social action, can ever be reduced to manageable levels. We cannot sustain the recent high growth rates. Yet it would be necessary to grow even faster if we wish to make a dent on our overwhelming debt.

To free us of this burden, we need to raise our rates of investment, in part by encouraging private domestic and foreign investment. In this regard, Paul Romer noted recently at a World Bank conference on the effect that national policies have in the long-run on growth, that the potential for rapid development through the transmission of ideas is great, but the problems of dividing up the surplus between industrial donors and developing recipients are considerable. There cannot be world recovery, prosperity and security when the Third World with 77% of the world's population now has 15% of the income, uses 12% of the natural resources and 18% of the energy.

This is a major issue that development banks should embrace, as they promote the private sector as the engine of growth. The interest of capital must not be put above humanity. This represents another area in which we need help in the shaping of our investment policies. The interests and viability of both the North and South depend on a genuine partnership and real interdependence, as was noted by Willy Brandt, Olaf Palme, Gro Harlem Bruntland, Julius Nyerere and others.

Decisive actions are necessary to bring about real solutions. The world as a whole cannot afford to go without a clear way forward. In a situation of confusion and uncertainty and with no solution in sight, the reactionary ultra-rightist/neo-fascists are getting stronger politically and becoming more vocal and strident. There is no answer to the hopelessness and desperation of the more than thirty million unemployed in the OECD countries. Despair is leading to alcoholism, narcotics, crime and suicide. Meanwhile, nationalism, xenophobia and neo-fascism are on the rise leading to racial-ethnic and growing civil strife.

The North/South dialogue has been languishing and has become a dialogue of the deaf. In the South, rising unemployment and abject poverty are interrelating and interacting with rapid growth of population, urbanization and overcrowding, diseases, the production and use of narcotic drugs, increased flows of refugees across international frontiers and an irreversible damage to the environment. Whereas before it was said that "Berlin Walls" prevented peoples in the former Soviet Union and Eastern Europe from travelling to the West, now new walls are being erected to prevent people from entering into the developed, industrialized countries.

It is not enough to treat the symptoms of the global malaise. Radical reforms are urgently needed. Structural adjustment is necessary for the developed countries as for the developing countries. But reforms must be predicated with social justice and have a human face. Human needs and human security should be the object of development. In this regard, greater emphasis should be placed on human capital and natural capital. And much more must be done to speed up disarmament so that the despairing and hungry of the world can benefit from greatly enhanced savings.

Let us now move fully towards the preparation of a development agenda by a panel of distinguished experts and experienced persons to prepare a practical report based on experience in diverse countries and on close, critical analysis of possible options. Such a report must deal with the international competitiveness of the Third World, the basis of new modalities for international co-operation for development and financing of development. It must also address core problems:

- the alleviation of poverty

- the expansion of productive employment
- the enhancement of social integration, particularly the more disadvantaged and marginal groups.

To attain these objectives, the people must play a central role. They must be fully involved in all aspects of life to take advantage of their initiative and creativity for the fashioning of a better future, a peaceful and prosperous world.

Basic Needs Strategy

A development strategy for the eradication of poverty must therefore be global and positive, not the South against the North and the North against the South, but the North and South in interdependence, co-operation and partnership.

In the present context of the shortage of funds, it is necessary to revisit the solution posed some years ago by the UN Conference on Disarmament and Development. Regrettably, because of Cold War considerations, no action was taken. It is now urgently necessary to move rapidly to cut military and other non-priority expenditures and utilize the "peace dividend" for the following:

1. Debt relief to the underdeveloped countries, such as Guyana, where about 80% of government revenues is allocated to payments of local and foreign debts and nearly 50% of foreign commercial earnings is utilized for the payments of a foreign debt of two billion dollars. Once debt relief is provided, funds will be available to lay the foundation for rapid economic growth, which can then provide the basis for the expansion of world trade through the purchase of goods and services, especially capital goods, from the developed countries;

2. A Works Program for physical and social infrastructure as was embarked upon by the Roosevelt New Deal Administration at the time of the Great Depression of the 1930s;

3. Increase employment by reducing the number of days or the number of hours worked per week, without loss

of pay, and the pensionable age without loss of benefits;

4. Tax and other incentives for the use of technology which will create jobs instead of destroying them. Science and technology (S&T) properly harnessed, has within its grasp the power of halving hunger by the end of this decade, and eradicating it by 2025. But this requires political will and a sound scientific strategy. Poverty will not be eliminated by "jobless growth."

There is urgent need for economic growth to be linked to social justice and eco-justice, human development, and the fullest exercise of all freedoms through good governance, efficient management and a basic needs development strategy.

Guyana: A Case for Debt Relief

Memorandum from President Cheddi Jagan to the Group of Seven Summit, Halifax, Canada.

For Guyana, a small country committed to the goals of sustainable development, social progress and a stable, transparent and participatory system of government, much is now at risk in the quest for attaining these very goals. Its people have labored for more than ten years under the crushing weight of an excessive external debt burden, the stock of which remains unsustainably high and the servicing of which presents an impossible challenge.

The circumstances confronting the country: its valiant effort to consolidate the gains of democracy; sustained effort at economic liberalization, economic policy reform through a program of structural adjustment; a cautious and prudent policy of environmental conservation and development, present a case for consideration of exceptional measures of debt relief by the donor community.

Debt Burden

Recognized by the World Bank as one of a number of severely indebted low income countries (SILICs) Guyana's external debt amounts to US$2.1 billion. The country subsists on a GNP per capita of below US$500. Its debt per capita amounts to approximately US$2,785, a sum five times its gross national product (GNP) per capita for 1994.

World Bank statistics revealed that Guyana's debt (in net present value terms) to export ratio is in excess of 300 per cent. In 1993, actual debt service to exports accounted for 24.5 per cent, while scheduled debt-service to exports (1991-93 average) amounted to 45.2 per cent. Actual debt service in 1993 recorded a transfer of US$90 million, in effect representing resources that are essential to promoting greater economic growth and meeting basic needs. To further illustrate the extent of the drain on an already impoverished economy, scheduled debt service payments for 1994 approximated US$131 million.

A casual assessment of these figures would make abundantly clear the severe debt overhang and liquidity crisis facing the country. The vicious cycle so created has meant that exiting from such a crisis would require an average annual economic growth rate of about fifteen per cent; the attainment of which, if at all possible, would be heavily dependent on a massive increase in export earnings. This in turn could only be made feasible with a large-scale injection of foreign capital, targeted at developing the productive bases and unleashing the country's substantial economic potential.

Thus far, debt rescheduling and consolidation, though beneficial, have not proved a lasting solution but rather have merely amounted to the postponement of a most critical problem. Economic reform programs with the IMF have been consistently adhered to and implemented, with acute risks of social and political instability. These reforms have been aimed inexorably at streamlining the management of the country's economy, improving productivity and competitiveness, creating an atmosphere of confidence for potential investors (foreign and local) and greater openness and economic liberalization.

But ultimately, the success or failure of these policy objectives hinge unfailingly on the degree of confidence inspired by the country's official relations with its creditors and other development partners. Admittedly, limited help has been realized, but officially, assistance of the proportions required for effectively dealing with the problem has been confined to the realm of hope with resource transfers, in 1993, accounting for a mere 11.6 per cent of GDP.

Possible Solutions

Inevitably, a conclusion drawn from the foregoing analysis is that Guyana's debt profile is of an unsustainable character under prevailing circumstances. The large and growing debt stock has resulted in a debt overhang that is the source of unmanageable servicing requirements. The persistence of the debt overhang will serve only to undermine confidence in the economy and in the policy objectives pursued by Government, a certain recipe for the discouragement of foreign investment and an invitation to capital flight.

Deriving from this, the first obvious solution to the country's economic woes is a considered reduction of its stock of debt. Here, what is being posited is not an elimination of the debt overhang. Debt reduction to a level that makes future debt servicing considerably more manageable will create room for greater economic flexibility on the part of Government, with greater openness, increased economic viability and the attraction of confidence by investors.

Additional concessional financing, whether in the form of grants or improved concessional flows, will have to accompany the two preceding actions in a complementary manner. Accelerated policy reforms and export-driven growth must be supported by immediate liquidity relief so as to attain their desired ends.

Guyana's debt is predominantly official and non-commercial (mainly bilateral and multilateral). Exceptional measures to reduce the debt stock, accompanied by the provision of new concessional financing will supplement and accelerate internal reforms and inevitably return the country to a path of self-sustained economic growth.

A Case For Relief

The case for urgent relief from Guyana's onerous debt burden is supported by arguments for political stability, social cohesion and environmental conservation.

Like several other states in the global community, Guyana's political system now rests on a fragile, fledging state of democratic governance. Its new government assumed power three years ago on a note of pervasive optimism, but was immediately challenged by problems of debt and servicing obligations and the potentially destabilizing consequences of on-going structural adjustment reforms.

The potential for political and social upheaval has in no way been dimmed since the transition to democratic change. A large measure of the underlying tensions would appear to stem from widespread dissatisfaction and disillusionment caused by the need for increased sacrifice to overcome a prolonged economic crisis. In the circumstances, it would be easy for the gains of democracy and stability to be over-turned or permanently retarded.

Furthermore, the fulfillment of its international obligations for ensuring environmental and ecological rectitude stands in direct conflict with the country's debt servicing requirements and its development needs. The principal means for achieving the latter two aims lie in the tremendous forestry, mineral and other natural resources capacity with which the country is endowed. Ultimately, the enhancement of export earnings, for those purposes, is heavily dependent on the development and exploitation of these and other productive sectors.

Nonetheless, a conscious decision to preserve such invaluable resources for the benefit of the global community constantly informs Government's policy regarding its other domestic and external obligations. For Guyana, the choice is therefore clear, namely, to continue its cautious, conservative approach to the use of its resources, at the expense of more rapid economic growth, or to pursue such growth by the full exploitation of the country's economic potential. The chosen option will be influenced in large measure by the degree of tangible support extended by the international community, particularly in the form of relief from the country's onerous debt burden.

The Quest for Peace, Justice and Development

Guyana's leader, President Cheddi Jagan was among 200 Heads of State who addressed the special commemorative meeting of the United Nation's General Assembly to mark the 50th anniversary of the world body.

In his presentation on October 24, 1995, President Jagan paid tribute to the work of the United Nations over the years, outlined the new tensions that threaten world peace and thwart development, and offered his own formula for a New Global Human Order.

As the United Nations proudly celebrates its fiftieth anniversary, I wish to join the other members of our international family in paying tribute to this organization which has served us so well over these many years.

As so many others before me have testified, the accomplishments of the United Nations during its fifty years of existence have been many and significant. With the ending of the Cold War, there is now a promise of even greater achievements. Yet although now free from the tensions of East-West rivalry, we are still hostage to many threats to our peace and security. This crucial time is characterized by:

• Globalization and liberalization with the dominance of transnational corporations (TNC's) and one overpowering ideology.

• Unacceptably high unemployment and underemployment, even in the period of economic growth, referred to as "jobless growth" and "jobless recovery."

• Increasing poverty and widening gaps in developed and developing countries, between the "haves" and the "have-nots," the "included" and the "excluded" and between the rich North and the poor South.

• Chronic budget and balance-of-payments deficit problems of many of the OECD countries are leading to the dismantling of the welfare state and cuts in welfare benefits in the North, and cuts in aid to the South - the phenomenon now deemed "donor fatigue" or "aid fatigue."

• Social, including family, disintegration.

• Strife and convulsions based on race, ethnicity, tribe, culture and religion leading to a marked increase in refugees.

• Demagogy and confusion, leading politically to the dangerous rise of the extreme right, the religious right, national chauvinists, xenophobists and neo-fascists, and socially to racism and racist attacks.

Cumulatively, these factors pose a grave threat to international and individual peace and security. Consequently, there is an urgent necessity for a New Global Human Order, as an adjunct to the UN Agenda for Development. A New Global Human Order must have as its goal human development: meeting the basic needs of the people, cultural upliftment, and a clean and safe environment.

To attain a New Global Human Order, it is necessary to establish a sound and just system of global governance based on:

• a genuine North/South partnership and interdependence for mutual benefit;

• a democratic culture of representative, consultative and participatory democracy and a lean and clean administration;

• a development of strategy free from external domination and *diktat*;

• application of science and technology for increased production and productivity;

• a global development facility, funded by pollution taxes, cuts in military expenditure - the peace dividend, which, with only a three per cent reduction can realize US$460 billion in a five-year period and a tax of 0.5 percent on speculative capital exchange movements, which can yield US$1500 billion annually;

• administration of a Development Fund by a democratized and reformed United Nations for allocation without undue conditions to the developed and developing countries. With such assistance, more job opportunities can be created by a works program, as under the Roosevelt New Deal Administration during the depression of the 1930s, a shorter workweek and a lower pensionable age. For the developing countries, aid can be given in the form of debt cancellation, long-term rescheduling of debt, soft loans and grants.

Third World debt is strangling our reconstruction and human development efforts. Although we paid more than US$1.3 trillion between 1982 and 1990, yet our countries were 61 percent more in debt in 1990 than they were in 1982. During the same period, there was a net South to North outflow of US$418 billion (not including outflows such as royalties, dividends, repatriated profits, underpaid raw materials, etc) - a sum equal to six Marshall Plans - the plan which provided aid to Europe at the end of World War II.

At the same time, our Third World countries lose annually, about US$500 billion in unfair, non-equivalent international trade, a sum equal to ten times ODA assistance from the developed countries.

This unjust economic order must be replaced by a just New Global Human Order for international and individual security and peace.

The human development paradigm must be established on the basis of empowerment of our peoples, accountability, productivity and sustainability.

Economic growth must be linked to equity, with social justice and ecological preservation.

Let us together resolve, on this historic occasion, to strengthen the United Nations which was created not only to preserve us from the scourge of war but also to allow our peoples to live in larger freedom.

I thank you.

Cheddi Jagan

Address to the Commonwealth Heads of Government Meeting in Auckland, New Zealand, November 9, 1995.

Presented by President Cheddi Jagan

I am particularly delighted to express the gratitude of the Commonwealth members from the Caribbean Community for the hospitality extended to our delegates. Our gratitude also goes out to the Secretary-General of the Commonwealth and his capable staff for the impeccable arrangements put in place for this important meeting.

Mr. Chairman, this is a very historic conference in that it heralds some revolutionary changes. Its significance is further enhanced with the return of South Africa to the Commonwealth. We also welcome Cameroon's presence among us. It is noteworthy that the advent of our 52nd Member State heralds a significant change in our cultural diversity.

The Caribbean Region is sensitive to all these changes and we are supportive of the initiatives to cross the cultural divide. However, this meeting bears greater significance as the Commonwealth observes serious contraventions to the theme and spirit of the Harare Declaration as it relates to good governance and human rights. Nevertheless, we are encouraged by the concerted efforts in place towards healing the blemishes.

The Commonwealth as an institution is uniquely placed to bridge the gap between the rich and poor nations, between the "haves" and the "have-nots." We in the Caricom sub-Region are faced with a huge foreign debt burden of US$10 billion, a continuing economic crisis with our principal exports experiencing difficulties in the international market-place and an inordinately high level of unemployment and under-employment. Mr. Chairman, we have implicit faith in the Commonwealth's ability to assist us with our debt problems.

We are pleased to note the definitive work undertaken by the Inter-governmental Group on the Global Humanitarian

Order. We are committed to this concept but on a wider development basis, called a New Global Human Order, which issue our Foreign Ministers at a recent meeting in New York, made a decision to address at all international fora.

In October 1985, Commonwealth Heads of Government issued the Nassau Declaration on World Order. At that time, member states were celebrating the fortieth anniversary of the United Nations. Ten years hence, there is a pressing need for us to reaffirm the principles upon which our Commonwealth organization has been founded - democracy, the rule of law and fundamental human rights - and in this fiftieth year of the birth of the UN, seek to consolidate the part which the Commonwealth can play within the international community to help combat the challenges to humanity.

There is need for a New Global Human Order which would provide for genuine North/South and East/West partnership and cooperation in the pursuit of this change.

Mr. Chairman, while all our countries are individually searching for more aggressive and innovative ways to cope with the growing inter-dependence and globalization taking place, there are fundamental issues which can be addressed only by new global initiatives. It is clear that as present worldwide trends continue, tensions, conflicts and disorders with potentially disastrous consequences can become the order of the day. Our concerns are real and are based on reality.

There is increasing poverty and widening gaps in the developed and developing countries, between the rich and the poor, the "haves" and the "have-nots," the "included" and the "excluded"; and the ever-growing gap between the North and the South.

Presently there is unacceptable high unemployment and under-employment even in the period of economic growth, referred to as "jobless growth"and "jobless recovery."

We witness budget and balance-of-payments deficit problems in the majority of the OECD states, leading to the dismantling of the welfare state and cuts in welfare benefits in the North, and cuts in aid to the South - the phenomenon now deemed "donor fatigue"or "aid fatigue." Added to this is the social, including family, disintegration.

In evidence is the vast increase in refugees due to the

prevalence of strife and convulsions based on race, ethnicity, tribe, culture and religion; also in evidence is the drug menace, money laundering, terrorism, crime, etc.

Dangerous trends are emerging: demagogy and confusion, leading politically to the rise of the extreme right, the religious right, national chauvinists, zenophobists and neo-fascists; and socially, to racism and racist attacks.

Cumulatively, these factors pose a grave threat to international and individual security and peace. As an adjunct to the UN Agenda for Development, a New Global Human Order must have as its goal human development: meeting the basic needs of the people; attaining cultural upliftment, and a clean and safe environment.

Our region, conscious of the emergence of free trade blocs in the hemisphere and beyond, and the enormous challenges for small developing countries like ours, has decided to put in place mechanisms effectively to treat our situation. At the last Meeting of Caricom Heads, held in Georgetown, Guyana, we decided on the establishment of a Regional Development Fund, as in the European Union. Such an initiative would ensure that developing states like ours are provided the opportunity to attain acceptable levels of development, which would allow us to compete hemispherically and in the wider international arena. The proposal is new and consultations have been on-going so as to refine and advance the concept.

The Caribbean has traditionally won acclaim as a Zone of Peace and we would crave your indulgence by requesting the Commonwealth's unswerving support for our efforts to retain this position, and request assistance in combating the additional ills of disease, corruption, narco-trafficking and money-laundering.

The Commonwealth has sought to formulate programs in crucial sectors in an endeavor to achieve a better quality of life for our people.

In particular, I wish to encourage those programs which focus on the support for women in the decision-making process and those which recognize the important role of young people in the national development process.

The contribution which the Commonwealth has made, and continues to make, in the provision of sustainable human development is a valuable one; in particular, the attention which it has paid to the security and developmental concerns of small states.

Guyana has received and continues to receive valuable forms of technical assistance. I wish in particular to express my sincere gratitude to the Secretary-General for the provision of urgently needed technical expertise following the spillage, in August this year, of over 2.5 million cubic feet of cyanide slurry into the Essequibo river - the largest river in Guyana - from the mining operations of the Omai Gold Mining Company.

This environmental disaster has heightened the need for developing countries to be better equipped to deal effectively with inherent environmental problems.

Small states need support to enhance their science and technology base. It is in this regard that I would like to commend the Commonwealth Science Council for the work which it has been conducting through science and technology programs to assist in capacity building, as well as human resource development in member countries.

Guyana values highly the assistance which it continues to receive from the Commonwealth in the development of the Iwokrama Rainforest Program, under which nearly a million acres of pristine rainforest in the hinterland of Guyana has been given to the world community for scientific research in the sustainable development of forest resources.

Mr. Chairman, I wish to congratulate His Excellency, Chief Emeka Anyaoku for the very effective and dynamic manner in which he has carried out his mandate, supported by a highly efficient Secretariat team.

I am confident that this setting will serve to inspire us as we deliberate over the path of the Commonwealth into the twenty-first century. I wish to borrow a quote from one of my Caricom colleagues and say *"Let us accentuate the positive. Let us build on what we have achieved and move forward as from today."*

Thank you.

Letter to Mr. James Wolfensohn President of the World Bank

Once again I want to take this opportunity to congratulate you on your new and exciting job as President of the World Bank. I had openly expressed my admiration of your immediate predecessor, Mr. Lewis Preston, for his forthright concern about world poverty and I have noticed from your background that you are equally concerned. I recall Mr. Maurice Strong of the World Resources Institute lauding your energetic advocacy of sustainable development and expressing his belief that your strong leadership style is needed at this critical stage in the history of the World Bank.

Since my PPP/Civic Administration took office, I have had cause on several occasions to pronounce on many of the burning issues facing Guyana, the Caricom region and the international community at large. Enclosed you will find a Memorandum I sent to Mr. M. Camdessus of the International Monetary Fund after he had met Caricom leaders in St Vincent, in which you will note some of our own concerns about poverty, debt and development. I am also enclosing a copy of a letter I had written to the G7 Heads of Government requesting that they support the initiatives of the British Government on debt, as expressed by that country's Chancellor of the Exchequer, particularly the debt owed by least-developed countries to multinational financial institutions.

We in Guyana are grateful for the assistance which we have been receiving from the World Bank and particularly from the IDA. However, our huge debt overhang inhibits our capacity to grow faster than we are doing, and to alleviate, if not eradicate, poverty.

Regrettably, the continuing and deepening crisis in the North (widening gap between the rich and poor; unacceptably high unemployment even in the period of economic recovery; social, including family disintegration), cuts in aid to the South, and globalization and liberalization are generally impacting adversely on the economies of the developing countries, including those in the Commonwealth Caribbean (Caricom).

In Guyana, with World Bank support, the state-owned LINMINE bauxite company was projected to attain profitability in 1994 and then be ready for privatization. Instead, the company, mainly as a result of external factors, lost US$10 million in spite of the fact that the State had assumed over US$40 million of its liabilities and employed an Australian management team.

In 1995, the US government cut its PL 480 title 3 wheat subsidy by 50 per cent.

Basic necessities like water, electricity, affordable housing, transport and roads, which are the indispensable ingredients for the creation of a favorable investment climate, are a daily hassle. Ironically, "in a land of many waters," with a very favorable land/population ratio, we suffer from land hunger in the densely-populated coastal plain and sometimes drought and floods occur in the same year! Trespassing and squatting have become a new plague and are giving rise to myriad social problems. We also have a weak physical and social infrastructure and inadequate administrative capacity.

Despite these serious constraints, my PPP/Civic government made remarkable progress. The Inter-American Development Bank in its 1993 annual report singled out Guyana for its "relatively successful stabilization and adjustment program" and credited it with the Caribbean's highest expansion rate, even as the sub-region experienced a growth rate of under one percent in 1993.

Real GDP grew by 7.7 percent in 1992, 8.3 percent in 1993, 8.5 percent in 1994 (highest in Latin America and the Caribbean), and 5.1 percent in 1995 (a drop from the targeted 6.3 percent because of the industrial disaster at the Omai Gold Mines Ltd.).

Consequently, an IDB Newsletter (June 1994, p. 10-11) described Guyana as a "small country with big economic ambitions" and "a shining example of a country on its way back from the abyss."

Economic growth would have been even more significant had it not been for serious reservations made by aid donors and environmentalists towards the granting of concessions to foreign investors, especially in the forestry sector, because of the monitoring incapacity of the Forestry Commission.

There remain many other continuing stumbling blocks, which include, according to IDB economist/consultant, Bertus J. Meins, "*Guyana's high external debt servicing obligations, continued fiscal deficits and as yet unmet needs for investment in maintenance and upgrading of physical infrastructure - a prime condition for attracting foreign investment in manufacturing. Also problematic is the country's weakly staffed public sector, which is involved in many productive activities but not enough to improve the human resource base.*"

We have done remarkably well in food production, particularly rice and sugar. We can become the "bread basket" for the food-short Caribbean, Latin America and the world, especially Africa, but we need to move rapidly with water-control, drainage and irrigation projects.

Unfortunately, project approval for loans and implementation is inordinately slow. Maybe, support for a Development Program, rather than individual projects, may render governments like mine the necessary speed and flexibility to solve more urgently pressing economic and social problems. As Marshall I. Goldman has noted with regard to reforms in Russia: "*...perhaps less attention should have been devoted to macro concerns;*" and, in countries like Guyana, more attention to capacity building and development of human resources.

Perhaps too, in the present global situation of increasing disorder and insecurity, expensive infrastructure costs, especially for agricultural development, should be borne by the international community, in the same way as the UNDP's 20/20 compact for social development.

Our greatest impediment, however, is our huge foreign debt of US$2.06 billion in 1995. How can we have economic, much less human, development with perhaps the highest per capita foreign debt? Our foreign debt payments of about US$112 million in 1995 was more than all capital inflows. We are caught in a vicious circle. Our people, over 40 percent below the poverty line, with a minimum wage in the public sector of about US$50 per month and a maximum salary of less than US$1000 per month, cannot physically, mentally and psychologically liberate Guyana from the vicious circle of poverty. The Guyana Trades Union Congress (GTUC) in a post-budget (1996) statement noted that the minimum wage was grossly inadequate and added that "*the market economy system which has been put in place here is not amenable to mechanisms that could cushion the impact of the [price] increases, noting that the price controls and subsidies are not permitted.*"

If we are to attain human development, then our foreign debt payments should not be more than 10 percent of our export earnings, as noted by a member of the delegation of the Global Governance Commission, Nobel Prize winner and former President of Costa Rica, Oscar Arias, to the Caricom Inter-Sessional Meeting in Belize in early 1995.

Imagine how much progress we could have made if, on the basis of this formula, our debt payments in the 1993-95 period were US$108.5 million, instead of US$308 million. With our vast resources, we could have doubled our existing generally high growth rate and moved significantly in the direction of eradicating poverty, which, according to the WHO, is the world's "deadliest disease."

At the Summit of the Americas, we agreed with the two major themes of democracy and free trade. But we added to the prescription for hemispheric ills the necessity for a Regional Development Fund, a Development Corps of Advisers and Specialists and Debt Relief.

It is within this context the warning of the Prime Minister of Dominica, Hon. Edison James, must be heeded: at a follow-up hemispheric meeting on Trade in Denver, he noted that if the banana producing countries of the Caribbean, some of which depend on bananas for about 70 per cent of their income, were to sink at the altar of free trade, then the citizens will have no alternative but to grow marijuana, or I may add, resort to crime and/or migrate to the North.

At the global level, the New World Order, after the Gulf War, has become a New World Disorder. In this regard, Susan George in her book *Debt Boomerang*, notes that if their world debt is not relieved, the boomerang will strike the North in a number of ways: environmental destruction, drugs, costs to taxpayers, lost jobs and markets, immigration pressures, heightened conflict and war.

What is needed, in the context of unacceptably high unemployment, even in the period of economic growth ("jobless recovery"), cuts in aid ("aid fatigue") and social disintegration, is a New Global Human Order, which my government is also advocating on the basis of genuine North/South partnership and cooperation in our interdependent world.

I do hope that the contributions of the USA and other countries to IDA would be increased, and the special World Bank facility contemplated for the least-developed countries will come into fruition. The World Bank has a crucial role to play, under your enlightened leadership, in eradicating poverty, safeguarding the environment and attaining sustainable human development.

In December 1992, the lead document of the Carnegie Commission on Science, Technology and Government for the Workshop on North/South Development Cooperation, called by President Jimmy Carter and UN Secretary-General Boutros Boutros-Ghali, noted that world hunger could be reduced by 50 per cent by the year 2000. Instead, as noted above, poverty has become the world's "deadliest disease." This comes at a time when science and technology afford us possibilities of not only alleviating but eradicating poverty.

Today, many governments, both collectively and individually, are earnestly searching for genuine solutions to fundamental problems facing our world. Regrettably, no answers are forthcoming. My New Global Human Order proposals to attain this objective include radical reforms embracing:

- The Roosevelt New Deal type of Works Program involving physical, social and cultural infrastructure in order to create more jobs as at the time of the 1930s depression;

- A reduction of the work week as mooted in Germany and France from 5 to 4 days or 40 to 35 hours in order to create more employment;

- Debt relief in the form of debt cancellation, long term rescheduling, grants and soft loans will cause greater economic growth in the South which in turn will help to access goods and services from the North, thus creating opportunities for more employment and stimulating world trade.

President Carter is assisting my Government in the preparation of a long-term development strategy. Our hope is to make Guyana a kind of model for other developing countries. In mid-April, I am hoping to present Guyana's case for urgent attention during a meeting in Atlanta arranged by the Carter Center.

The European Union has already given recognition to Guyana as an example of good governance for sustainable human development. After my address to the Economic Committee of the European Parliament and discussions with the leaders of the European Commission, Guyana obtained additional assistance amounting to six million ECU's; and the then Commissioner of Economic Cooperation, Manuel Marin appealed to the Presidents of the IMF and World Bank to examine sympathetically our debt problem.

I look forward to your meeting with the Caricom Heads of Government and your solidarity and support for the world's poor, marginalized, oppressed and suppressed.

Yours Sincerely,

Cheddi Jagan
President, Republic of Guyana
February 12, 1996.

Guyana's National Development Strategy

Paper presented by Dr. Cheddi Jagan at the Global Development Initiative (GDI) Advisory Group Meeting held at The Carter Center, Atlanta, Georgia on June 6, 1996.

Ladies and gentlemen, on behalf of my Government and the people of Guyana, I wish to thank you for attending this very important meeting. I believe it will prove to be very worthwhile for us to have this opportunity to converse about Guyana's vision of its development and our new social and economic policies that will be guiding it.

I wish especially to thank President Jimmy Carter for organizing this event and for his valuable assistance to our National Development Strategy over the past year. He is a steadfast friend of Guyana who always is motivated by the noblest aims.

We also acknowledge the support of the international community, manifested in the recent decision of the Paris Club to write off one-fourth of our debt. All Guyana is grateful for this gesture and is filled with hope over the prospects that it raises. We know the road ahead still is difficult, and that careful debt management will be required. But now some of the heavy burdens of the past that have been blocking our path are at last being removed. However, debt servicing will continue to impose severe constraints in the medium-term because debts that were previously not being honored would have to be serviced now.

I hope that in our inter-dependent world, North/South partnership and co-operation for mutual benefit would lead to the conclusion of Third World debt payments not exceeding, annually, 10 percent of income from exports, as advocated by Nobel Prize Winner and former President of Costa Rica, Oscar Arias, former President of Zambia, Dr. Kenneth Kaunda, the British Labor Party and others.

Overview of the National Development Strategy

The agenda for today is our National Development Strategy:

how it has been developed, the policy orientations it puts forth and, above all, what it means for Guyana and the donor community.

I would like to take this opportunity to comment on the context out of which the National Development Strategy arose and the broad vision that it paints of our economy and society.

In broad terms, this is a unique, forward-looking, creative vision. It is development with a human face. It addresses frankly our most basic social problems, including health, education, housing, poverty concerns, the role of women, and the role of Amerindians. It is committed to honor fully the UN Covenant on Civil and Political Rights and the UN Covenant on Economic, Social and Cultural Rights, to foster unity in diversity and to provide for accelerated development of our indigenous Amerindian people.

The strategy defines both new responsibilities as well as opportunities. It places great expectations on the private business sector. At the same time it fosters wider citizen participation in basic decisions by enabling local governments, citizens associations, labor unions, farmers' groups, co-operatives and NGOs to play enhanced roles. It seeks to devolve responsibility to its most appropriate level.

Central Government will achieve greater effectiveness by concentrating its role more in guidance and oversight in establishing basic policies and monitoring their implementation. And the Government, as amply demonstrated in the Development Strategy, considers the private sector as the engine of economic growth. Public perception that privatization of state entities was conducted in a less that transparent manner dictated that we move cautiously.

We believe that the Government of a developing economy must exercise strong leadership. The State must constantly be alert to represent the interests of the population at large, and it must be an effective steward of our rich endowment of natural resources. This is a powerful role. But it is best exercised through instruments of policy, and specialized programs to complement the efforts of the private sector.

The National Development Strategy, which is still in draft but will be released shortly, is an exceptional document in respect of both the process of formulating it and the nature of the document. The process has been unusually participatory; in the first stage, more than 200 national experts have contributed considerable amounts of time to developing technical diagnoses of issues and preliminary sets of policy options in each area. Subsequent stages will involve consultations with a wide gamut of groups and institutions in our society before the document is finalized. Few countries can claim to have developed a national socio-economic strategy through a participatory process.

The Strategy is distinguished by being both broad and deep. The various chapters cover all sectors and all key topics of economic policy and social programs, and the policies established in preliminary form in each chapter are firmly buttressed by thorough technical analyses.

The Strategy takes a long-term view of our country's growth prospects and requirements, and the special needs of less favored groups in society, and on that basis it establishes firm foundations for continuing improvements in the standard of living of all Guyanese.

The Social and Historical Context of the Strategy

I believe this National Development Strategy will come to be regarded as an historic document for our country, and for that reason it needs to be viewed in the light of our history. Guyana's first decades of Independence have been its crucible of nationhood in political, social and economic respects. These have been intense and difficult years in many respects, yet out of the struggles and self-examination a sense of self-identity and a modern nation are emerging, in measured steps but assuredly.

The nation's polity had to be defined against the backdrop of a population brought to our shores in disenfranchised conditions and cleavages wrought in the society by colonial rule. Global geopolitical tensions also left their imprint on the nascent body politic. Throughout these lacerating historical experiences, the spirit of nationhood has deepened, although at times it has appeared to fray under the pressures, it has shown resilience.

The elections of the year 1992 marked a political watershed in consolidating the spirit and confirming the country's commitment to the path of democracy. We are still a very young nation and our fundamental political and social values are still being forged, and we therefore look to the future with more confidence than at any time in our brief history.

Permit me to thank President Carter, President Bush, the US Congress, the NDI, Brian Atwood and others for the tremendous assistance they rendered in restoring democracy to Guyana.

For me, democracy is the life-blood of human development: a democracy which is representative, consultative and participatory and embraces the political, economic, industrial, social and cultural spheres.

The progress of the economy largely mirrored that of the polity. Until recently, real per capita incomes declined, poverty was on the increase and health and educational standards fell while the nation's infrastructure deteriorated. Many of Guyana's brightest talents chose to emigrate rather than continue to suffer the straitened circumstances of the domestic economy. Developing human resource and social capital will be one of our principal tasks.

Lack of democracy, falling external terms of trade and inappropriate domestic economic policies played their role in the economic decline, including a willingness to incur a crushing burden of external debt that has reached unserviceable levels.

The benefits of the new policies have begun to become apparent. In the last four years, Guyana has experienced a turn-around in its economic performance that is remarkable by any standard. After a decade in which real growth rates were on average negative, the economy has registered real growth averaging about seven percent per year for the past three years. These positive developments have led to a diminution of unemployment rates and a lessening of poverty, although both those issues remain matters of considerable national concern.

Our strategy is geared to attaining high sustainable economic growth with equity - growth with social justice and ecological preservation.

At the same time that the economy was taking off, the government budget deficit and the balance of payments deficit were reduced, inflation was brought down sharply, and the arrears on external accounts were diminished very substantially.

Although many daunting problems still confront Guyana, these economic changes have begun to lay the basis for sustained growth and balanced urban-rural development. They also have generated a more optimistic spirit, and the beginnings of a renewal of faith in the country's future can be perceived. Hope and confidence are indisputable for social progress, as are a sound development strategy and plan, international co-operation, and good governance - democratic, lean and clean.

As encouraging as recent developments have been, the obstacles that remain in the path of development are large, and redoubled efforts are required to overcome them. The difference from a decade ago is that now we know they can be solved with wise policies, persistence, and a national democratic state of all classes and strata, with the working class not dominating but not being dominated, to ensure economic growth with equality.

Those obstacles include not only hindrances to the expansion of production but also deteriorated social services and a governmental structure that is weakened in its ability to set and enforce the basic rules of the economy. They include both decayed physical infrastructure and institutions that still do not function up to expectations. We are worried about external market conditions for our basic agricultural products, fully aware that they may change for the worse, providing lower returns to our workers and farmers by the beginning of the new century. Our bauxite communities are experiencing difficulties as a result of the external environment, and especially the unfavorable conditions in the global bauxite/aluminum market-place. The challenges are many and diverse.

The manifold nature of the problems that lie ahead, and the increasing complexity of our economy, have dictated that we undertake to formulate a multi-faceted strategy for overcoming the problems. Macro-economic policy sets the overall framework, but policy also has a sectoral expression, and it must not be forgotten that the economy responds at the micro level, which is the human level.

For these reasons the Strategy has very specific content, including detailed recommendations for reforms in the existing legislative framework that would be needed to facilitate the implementation of the policies.

While no policy planning document achieves all its aims, this Strategy and its policies are strong and sure enough to carry forward our rapid economic expansion for another ten years, if not more, and make our citizens measurably better off whilst assuring that our priceless heritage of natural resources has proper stewardship.

Basic Themes of the Strategy

To achieve our ultimate goal of people-centered development, we need to pursue rapid growth - the main source of employment creation - at the same time that we intensify our endeavors to alleviate poverty. We need to improve our population's access to basic social and economic services, and we need to encourage participation by all segments and sectors of society.

We are committed to economic growth, as the only way to realize the most basic aspirations of our population, but we are also committed to equitable growth. There are two basic approaches to poverty alleviation. One is temporary subsidies to enable the lower income groups to have access to sufficient amounts of food and other basic necessities, and the other is creation of an economic environment that will enable them to secure those necessities through exertion of their own abilities. The latter is the course we have chosen to emphasize, although the former approach is a necessary complement in the interim, until the income-earning capacities of the poor are expanded sufficiently.

In the long-run the aim is clear, as I have expressed on earlier occasions, we are ultimately more concerned with the strengthening of self-reliance, the eradication of poverty at its roots, rather than with handouts to relieve poverty. Our development path also must be characterized by the three kinds of sustainability: fiscal, institutional and environmental. Quick fixes in these areas are doomed to failure, with damaging consequences.

We are an economy rich in natural resources, and those sectors can be expected to continue to expand, but a narrowly-based growth path is risky, and the desired level of social and economic development cannot be attained on the basis of a few primary products alone. We need to diversify our economy and to develop our own new specializations that will be internationally competitive and enduring. It is essential that we continuously improve productivity in all sectors.

Above all, we need to strengthen our base of human resources and mesh human resource development with Guyana's vast natural resources. Among other measures this means improving social infrastructure, providing higher public sector wages, and giving more emphasis to training programs for the labor force.

During the past three years, my government has doubled expenditure in the social sector, and at the UN Social Summit at Copenhagen, I pledged to increase expenditure to 20 percent in keeping with the 20/20 UNDP Compact. I hope the international community will respond appropriately.

The strategic orientations of keys to rapid growth for Guyana are three-fold: export growth, savings mobilization, education and training. Expressed in the terminology of economics, this is expansion of markets for our products, mobilization of the necessary financial capital, and improvement of our base of human capital. All three orientations are indispensable elements of our growth strategy.

A Basis for International Co-operation

For Guyanese, we believe this Strategy will come to signify faith in the future, and in our ability to work together as a multi-ethnic society to achieve betterment for all. It marks the first time that Guyanese of all races, religions and political persuasions have come together to draft a blueprint for our future.

For the international community, this Strategy initiates a fruitful dialogue and marks the beginning of a new era in co-operation. We believe this Strategy should be the point of departure for programming international assistance. It establishes the policy framework that we would like to see supported and the areas of priority actions.

We do not ask or expect agreement on every aspect. That would be unrealistic to ask of anyone, Guyanese or foreigner. But we do ask that the document be taken into serious consideration in the planning of international technical and financial support. In this regard, we ask for respect for a poor country's right to play a major role in charting its own future course, and a collaborative spirit in moving the country along that course. Detailed implementation plans will be drawn up in each area of action and we invite collaboration in that effort as well.

I would like at this point to crave your indulgence to share with you my vision of how I see Guyana within the wider perspective of global development. It is well known that I have been calling, like many world leaders, for radical changes in the present world disorder and for a New Global Human Order.

This advocacy is premised on the fact that in this era of globalization and liberalization, we cannot be an "island unto ourselves." Whether we like it or not, the world impinges on us in the South and more often than not adversely, especially small island and small economy states as in the Caribbean Community.

With Free Trade mooted for 2005, these countries face marginalization, unless the proposals I made at the Miami Summit of the Americas in December 1994 for a Regional Development Fund, debt relief, and a Corps of Development Specialists, are seriously considered. Regrettably, signals thus far indicate that they would not be realized. Also, not being realized is the expectation of the Report of the Carnegie Commission on Science, Technology, and Government presented at the workshop here in December 1992, that with the level of scientific and technological advances, it was possible to reduce hunger by 50 percent by the year 2000. Regrettably, the opposite is taking place. The poverty curtain is widening the gap in living standards between the rich and the poor in the South as well as the North, and between the North and South, is ever widening. The specter of unemployment, poverty and social disorder is haunting the world. And at the political level, there is the dangerous and growing ascendancy of the far right, ultra-nationalists, fundamentalists, xenophobists and neo-facists, reminiscent of Hitlerism. Regrettably, no lasting solutions are forthcoming while the world is clamoring for stability, peace and security. I think there are solutions. We must show the will and the courage to adopt them and make the world a better place. While we focus on our individual countries we have to make the world environment more responsive to the needs of those countries which are now on the road to progress. As we say in Guyana, "*Think Globally! Act Locally!*"

In former times of crises, new initiatives were taken - the Keynes formula of pump-priming the economy during the down-turn of the business cycle (depression/recession) - as adumbrated in the Roosevelt New Deal Works Program, the Marshall Aid Plan to devastated Europe at the end of the Second World War, the Alliance for Progress for Latin America and the Caribbean, the Lome Convention for the African /Caribbean/ Pacific (ACP) countries.

The present critical time, calls for the setting up of an agency like the United Nations Relief and Rehabilitation Agency (UNRRA) headed by New Dealer Fiorello La Guardia, to cope with the wartime ravages and the problems of reconstruction.

This would mean also the creation of a separate Development Fund, especially in this period of "jobless growth" and "jobless recovery" in the North, and aid cuts (aid fatigue) to the South. This D-Fund should be disbursed to both the states of the North and the South. In the North for a New Deal type of works program, for a reduction of the work week without loss of take home pay and the reduction of the pensionable age without loss of benefits, in the south, for debt relief and enhanced Alliance for Progress and Lome Convention programs.

The D-Fund can be created from cuts in global military expenditures, pollution taxes, the Tobin tax on speculative capital movements and a small airline ticket tax on long distance flights.

Perhaps, this Global Development Initiative Meeting should consider establishing a separate top level Commission on Sustainable Development and the Environment to formulate a global strategy and plan of action.

In closing, I would like to mention two particular areas in which a unique form of international co-operation could be very beneficial to Guyana, and perhaps also to other countries with similar kinds of resource endowments.

First, the Strategy lays out a very vigorous program of strengthening our sustainable management of natural resources. This is the only way to guarantee to future generations of Guyanese the opportunities that are being offered to the present generation. We are concerned to establish ways to make economic development compatible with sound management of natural resources. In this regard, we would like to call your attention to the proposal to establish a Guyana Rainforest Foundation. Such a foundation would play a major role in promoting sustainable management of our unique heritage of extensive rainforest. It would finance and manage non-timber concessions in the forest, developing activities such as research, eco-tourism and protection for bio-diversity on those lands. Exclusive rights to manage concessions in that way would be granted upon agreement to remit royalties per acre just as a timber concession would.

We feel this is a most promising avenue to pursue, for other countries as well, because it combines the need for development finance with the environmental aims for tropical forests. A proposal for the Foundation is now being drafted, and we hope to interest donors, including bilateral official donors, international NGOs and corporations. The second special opportunity that the National Development Strategy identified for international co-operation is the development of centers of excellence at the University of Guyana. Only one or two such centers would be created each decade, starting with fields such as geology and mining, or tropical forestry and wood products industries.

We feel it is vital to develop the best scientific expertise in fields like these, to support our sustainable development path. The centers would emphasize research and teaching, and would maintain close links to NGOs and industries in their respective fields. Again, we would like to solicit the interest of donors, from official entities to corporations, and enlist the co-operation of leading universities abroad in this pioneering effort.

Ladies and gentlemen, I look forward to a fuller discussion of our National Development Strategy when it is finalized, and I thank you for your attention today.

Address to the Conference on a New Global Human Order, Georgetown, Guyana

Under the auspices of the Government of Guyana, a Conference was held from August 2-4, 1996, at the Auditorium of the Sophia National Exhibition Park, Georgetown, Guyana, to discuss the creation of a New Global Human Order.

Participants included progressive thinkers and social activists from both developed and developing countries as well as a cross section of Guyanese society.

In his inaugural address to the Conference, Dr. Cheddi Jagan, President of Guyana, adumbrated his concept for a New Global Human Order.

This Conference is being held at a crucial juncture in historical and human development.

The scientific and technological revolution and the information revolution have transformed our world to the point where mankind is in a position to expect universal prosperity. However, this great promise, especially with the ending of the sharp ideological/political confrontation of the coldwar period, to meet man's basic needs and to provide individual and international security is far from being fulfilled. Indeed, even as recently as the end of the Gulf War, President George Bush proclaimed a New World Order and an era of peace and tranquillity.

But regrettably, instead of order there is now grave disorder worldwide, because of the paradox of the continued development of the forces of production on the one hand and the increasing deterioration of the quality of life on the other - growing poverty and increasing inequality.

Megablocs with powerful economic centers exist along with countries just emerging from industrialization, while others, mainly in the so-called Third World, continue to be agricultural. It is obvious that with globalization based on liberalization, those who are lagging behind in modernization, will face marginalization and its consequent dangers. And these dangers are already manifesting themselves in a variety of ways.

Poverty

The gap in living standards between the rich and the poor in both the North and the South is getting wider: the rich, "the included," "the haves," are getting richer at the expense of the poor, "the excluded," "the havenots."

According to the United Nations, 1.2 billion people in the Developing World live in absolute poverty, almost double 1984 figures, and hunger (over half of sub-Saharan African children are starving or malnourished and diseased). UNICEF and UNDP figures show that over six million children under the age of five had died each year since 1982 in Africa, Asia and Latin America.

The late World Bank President, Lewis T. Preston, told the UN Conference on Population and Development that two billion people were without clean water, and three million children died each year from malnutrition.

Note these alarming facts:

• Each year 13 million children under five worldwide, still die from easily preventable diseases and malnutrition.

• There are nearly 200 million moderately to severely malnourished children under five in developing countries - 36 per cent of all children in this age group. Some 69 million are severely malnourished.

In developing countries, 130 million children, almost two thirds of them girls, lack access to primary education.

"*In a world where we now talk about gross domestic product of tens of billions of dollars*," observed James P. Grant, the late Executive Director of the United Nations Children's Fund, "*to have children deprived of basic education, health care and minimal amounts of food is increasingly obscene. Morality must change with capacity*."

In Latin America, there is economic growth but persistent poverty. In a letter to *The York Times* (December 5, 1993) it was pointed out that Juan de Dias Parra, leader of the Latin American Association for Human Rights, summarized the recent trends at a meeting in Quito, Ecuador, noting that "*in Latin America today, there are 70 million more hungry, 30 million more illiterate, 10 million more families without homes and 40 million more unemployed persons than there were 20 years ago... There are 240 million human beings who lack the necessities of life and this when the region is richer and more stable than ever, according to the way the world sees it.*"

Poverty is even likely to increase. As of 1986, 37 per cent of the region's families were living in poverty: by 2000, the UN Economic Commission on Latin America and the Caribbean (ECLAC) estimates that between 40 per cent to 60 per cent of the population would be below the poverty line!

"*The coming years will be quite difficult for these countries,*" said Peter Jenson, ECLAC Coordinator for Human Settlements. "*Growth has been really on only one end of the spectrum, the wealthy. The rich are getting richer and the poor are getting poorer. And this will generate social conflict.*"

In Africa, the number of the most critical least-developed countries has increased.

Sir Neville Nicholls, President of the Caribbean Development Bank (CDB), estimates that one-third of the population of the Commonwealth Caribbean is living in poverty.

Meanwhile, the gap in living standards between the highly industrialized North and the undeveloped South is ever-widening.

The North has roughly one-fifth of the world's population and four-fifths of its income, and it consumes 70% of the world's energy, 75% of its metals and 85% of its wood.

Unemployment

The Achilles heel of globalization and liberalization is unemployment.

About 800 million people from a global labor force of 2.8 billion are unemployed or under-employed - the largest proportion being in the working age population which is outside the labor force.

During the next 30 years, the global labor force will increase from 2.8 billion to about 3.8 billion. In the developing countries it will be necessary to create about 40 million new jobs annually, just to cope with the growing labor force, in addition to the jobs for the gainful employment of the presently unemployed or under-employed.

The "politically-explosive" unemployment figure in the OECD industrialized countries is now 36 million, with 20 million in Europe alone. The IMF projects only a small decline in the European Union unemployment rate from an average 11.8 per cent in 1994 to 11.5 per cent in 1995, the highest level since the 1930s.

During the past few decades, levels of unemployment were linked more to cyclical than to structural factors - decreases during upturns in the economy, and increases during downturns. However, Mihaly Simai says it was the recession of the early 1990s, and the patterns of recovery from it, which revealed the increasingly structural sources of unemployment. *"Unemployment rates ballooned, and the number of long-term unemployed increased. The resultant social costs of unemployment reached new heights; in 1994, the annual cost of unemployment in the European Union, including income losses, exceed [sic] US$200 billion. About two thirds of this amount was spent on unemployment benefits."*

"Jobless growth" and "jobless recovery" have now become a structural feature not only of the European Social Market Model of monopoly capitalism but also the American Model.

In the 1950s and 1960s, a 2-3 per cent unemployed was regarded as the norm in the capitalist industrial states: now, the percentage has increased to 4-5 percent. In Europe, it is more than double.

Keith A. Bezanson, President of the International Development Research Centre (IDRC), in Canada, says that the globalized marketplace is shifting some jobs to the South, and *"that shift is making the discarded workers of the North poorer and very, very angry,"* as was demonstrated particularly in France in recent times. And with more workers being put on the dole, there is little room for work for the graduates of colleges and universities. Bezanson estimates that by the year 2015, *"around 700 million new job seekers will be entering the labour market in one year alone. 700 million! That figure is staggering when we realize that less than 50 million will knock on the doors of the global labour market this year."*

A perspective study by ECLAC for Latin America for the 1985-95 period predicted an increase in poverty and a doubling of the unemployment rate.

In the Caribbean sub-region, social problems are becoming acute. Nearly a decade ago the "Twelve Wise Men," headed by Nobel Prize Laureate, Sir Arthur Lewis, had noted high unemployment in some territories of nearly 30 per cent and warned that it could become an explosive problem. Referring to the present situation, the President of the Caribbean Development Bank, Sir Neville Nicholls, asserted: *"The generally weak performance of the economies did little to relieve the serious unemployment situation. About 200,000 working age West Indians across the region remained jobless in 1993, many of them young people and women. There was the consequential continued rise in social problems and the governments just did not have the resources with which to finance compensatory activities that would provide more jobs."*

In a report to the Caricom Summit in Barbados in July 1994, the Caribbean Association of Industry and Commerce (CAIC) referred to the growing jobless figures and declining levels of foreign aid and investment. On unemployment and underemployment, the CAIC said these levels remained far too high:

"(They) do not begin to tell, in their cold statistical reciting, either the tragedy of broken lives and wasted human potential in our region, but also speak of a problem which, if not solved or at least significantly ameliorated, will ultimately destroy, through industrial and societal disruption, all other well-meaning efforts at economic development."

Disintegration

Unemployment is not only degrading. It is also linked to poverty, hunger, social disintegration, family dislocation, environmental degradation, desertification, narcotrafficking, urbanization, migration, crime and conflict.

East/West confrontation, based on ideology, has given way to conflicts rooted in racial/ethnic, religious and cultural/historical differences both between and within states.

Coupled with population growth and mass migration, poverty and insecurity are posing the dangers of an equally-terrifying political explosion, as seen in Somalia, Rwanda, Burundi, the former Yugoslavia, the Middle East and elsewhere.

As a result of global poverty, convulsions and conflicts, more than 100 million migrants are living outside their countries of origin. Some 19 to 23 million of these are refugees or in refugee-like situations - up from 3.5 million in 1985. In addition, about 26 million people are internally displaced within their own countries. These figures show no sign of abating but rather are growing!

The United Nations peace-keeping operational expenditures increased seven-fold between 1991 and 1992, whilst UN agencies' aid programs declined by ten per cent between 1992 and 1993.

In the industrialized countries, drugs and crime have become serious problems. Today, roughly half of US households possess arms, and every year about 38,000 persons die of gunshots.

Jingoism and xenophobia are raising their ugly heads. Across the globe, the neofascists, the conservative far right and the religious far right are gaining ground politically.

The Commonwealth Caribbean, long recognized for its democratic traditions, is stagnating and facing a crisis not known since the late 1970s when the Caribbean Basin was deemed as one of the "circles of crisis."

Debt Crisis

Debt stultifies development. It leads to underdevelopment. This in turn leads to unemployment, under-employment, poverty, social and family disintegration, hunger, illiteracy, juvenile delinquency, crime, suicide and emigration.

Third World debtor countries paid more than US$1.3 trillion between 1982 and 1990, yet in 1990, they were 61 per cent more in debt than they were in 1982.

Since the early 1980s, the Latin American and Caribbean countries have honored their debt obligations at tremendous suffering of the masses of the people. Yet, the debt continues to grow.

According to the 1992 UNICEF publication, "*Children of the Americas:*" Between 1981 and 1990 Latin America spent US$503 billion on foreign debt payments (US$313 billion in interest). At the same time, the regions consolidated external debt rose from US$297 billion in 1981 to US$428 billion in 1990. This mechanism whereby "they more you pay the more you owe" is perverse and must be stopped.

The $10 billion (US) debt of the Commonwealth Caribbean countries imposes a crushing burden and inhibits sustainable development.

Susan George in her book, **The Debt Boomerang,** pointed out that in the 1982-1990 period, according to the Organization of Economic Cooperation and Development (OECD), total resource flows - all official bilateral and multilateral aid, grants by private charities, trade credits plus direct private investment and bank loans - from the developed North to the developing countries amounted to US$927 billion.

At the same time, there was a US$1,345 billion net overflow in the form of debt service alone. *"For a true picture of resource flows, one would have to add many other South-to-North outflows such as royalties, dividends, repatriated profits, underpaid raw materials and the like. The income-outflow difference between $1,345 and $927 billion is thus a much understated $418 billion in the rich countries' favour. For purposes of comparison, the US Marshall Plan transferred $14 billion in 1948 dollars to war-ravaged Europe, about $70 billion in 1991 dollars. Thus in the eight years from 1982-90 the poor have financed six Marshall Plans for the rich through debt service alone."*

In a letter to the World Bank President, James Wolfenson, I pointed out that *"Guyana's foreign debt payments of about US$112 million in 1995 was more than all capital inflows. We are caught in a vicious circle. Our people, over 40 per cent below the poverty line, with a minimum wage in the public sector of about US$50 per month and a maximum salary of less than US$ 1,000 per month, cannot physically, mentally and psychologically liberate Guyana from the vicious circle of poverty."*

I went on to point out that Guyana's external debt payments in the 1993-95 period were US$308 million. But if a formula of 10 per cent of export income was used, the debt payments would have been only US$108.5 million. In such a situation, this small economy state would have made significant progress to improve the quality of life and to advance physical and social infrastructure development, and thus prepare a more conducive atmosphere for private investment, foreign and local.

The huge foreign debt and huge drain of funds contribute to Third World poverty, the world's "deadliest disease," according to the WHO.

The process of accumulation and export of capital (hard currency) had led to the average citizen of the low-income debtor country being 55 times poorer, and the average citizen of a middle-income country 9 times poorer than the average citizen of the OECD creditor country - "*this process has been justifiably likened to extracting blood from a stone.*"

Fiona Godlee, assistant editor of the British Medical Journal, in an article, "**The World Debt Drains Third World Health**" in 1994, says: "*Third World debt holds back world economic recovery, increases the spread of disease, feeds the international traffic in drugs, damages the environment, and increases political instability and civil war, thus adding to the global refugee crisis.*"

Structural Adjustment

IMF/World Bank Structural Adjustment Programs, though necessary in cases of grave economic/fiscal problems, have not produced the desired results in many countries.

Condemning the "trickle-down" economic policies of the IMF, US Congressman Bernie Sanders observed that its adjustment policies "*actually exacerbate the plight of the poor.*" He attacked the "harsh" requirements of the structural adjustment program of the IMF and World Bank, saying that "*after 50 years, we should see the benefits of our investments. Instead, we are seeing the rich get richer while the poor fall deeper into poverty.*"

The major concern of the IMF/World Bank structural adjustment program, says Susan George, is to accumulate hard currency by increasing exports and reducing government outlays – "*earn more and spend less.*" The main aim is to "*make sure the debt is serviced.*"

As regards structural adjustment and reforms, **The State of the South** pointed out: "*However, in the adjustment process of the 1980s, these needed reforms were frustrated by an* *unbalanced international approach towards structural adjustment and by the conditionality prescribed by the international financial institutions. The macro-economic policies – in particular fiscal and exchange rate policies – virtually forced upon developing countries as part of programs for stabilization and structural adjustment were geared to achieving a quick, short-term improvement in the balance of payments. Safeguarding the interests of international commercial banks even at the cost of a severe economic contraction thus became the primary concern of international strategy on debt management."*

Further, the programs for stabilization and adjustment pressed upon developing countries did not provide for sufficient external financial support to permit adjustment to occur and endure without choking their growth. The programs were based on unduly optimistic assumptions about the speed at which structural maladies could be corrected. In addition, they were generally shaped by a doctrinaire belief in the efficacy of market forces and monetarist policies. This combination of priorities and policies aggravated the developing countries' economic woes and social distress in a number of ways."

Free Trade

Economic globalization and liberalization, with the dominance of the transnational corporations and one over-powering ideology, are linked to the free movement of capital, goods and services, market dominance and threats to sovereignty and security, especially of small states.

A good example is the United States banana marketing giant, Chiquita Brands, which has objected to the European Banana Import Regime.

For the Windward Islands - Dominica, Grenada, St. Lucia and St. Vincent and the Grenadines, bananas account for approximately half of total export earnings, 15 per cent of total production (Gross Domestic Product) and employ some 13 per cent of the labour force.

In Dominica, for example, over 70 per cent of the total export earnings come from bananas. The industry earns some US$200 million annually for the Region.

The Chiquita monopoly whose annual sales of US$2.5

billion is six times the GDP of St. Lucia, one of the four Windward Islands, is supported by other marketing giants such as Dole Fruits and Del Monte. It wants, on the gospel of free trade, to capture the three per cent ACP share of world banana exports.

Globalization and liberalization are leading to the reversal of all trends towards fairness and justice, growing misery of people excluded from work, from social space and socially recognized life, says Ronald J. Schlesander in his "*The Frankfurt School Critique of Capitalist Culture*."

The industrial countries continue to maintain their protectionism which was the basis of their economic growth and development. Up to World War I, the prevailing practice was "islands of liberalism surrounded by a sea of protectionism" for the North and "an ocean of liberalism with islands of protection" for the South. This led to deindustrialization of the Third World. Between 1860 and 1913, the developing countries' share of world manufacturing production declined from over one-third to under a tenth. And the target of 20 per cent by the year 2000 will not be met.

Under the present globalized agenda, not only the gospel of liberalization and free trade are being peddled, but also the UN Transnational Agency has been scrapped and UNIDA and UNCTAD are under threat of liquidation.

Meanwhile, in keeping with the trend of economic liberalization, the Caricom Summit agreed in late 1992 to lower the common external tariff (CET): 40 per cent in 1992; 30 per cent in 1996 and 20 per cent in 1998.

And the Summit of the Americas agreed in December 1994 to free trade in the Western Hemisphere by 2005.

Already, there are signals of crisis. Barbados, nearly a decade ago, had ten factories producing components for the North American market. Now, there are only three. Some of the small Windward OECS island states are not implementing the CET for fear of its impact on the people. Trinidad complains of a conspiracy to block its exports by Barbados and some other Caricom countries. And because of cheaper imports, Guyanese farmers including Amerindians, in two large regions — the North West Region One near to Venezuela and the Rupununi Region Nine near to Brazil — cannot sell their peanuts.

Deregulation of imports and subsidies in Jamaica exacted its toll on local manufacturers and farmers.

Many questions are being raised about the indecisiveness of Caricom leaders and their inability to fulfill decisions and to arrive at a Single Market and Economy. What really should be questioned is the *raison d'être* of the integration movement and the strategy of development adopted by Carifta and Caricom.

Flawed Models

The fierce competition, between the world capitalist centers with computers and robots, is creating contradictions and innumerable problems: the trickle-down process does not work. We need our own agenda - a new agenda of sustainable human development. Past "models" of development have proven to be wanting. Capitalism's market-driven neo-liberalism for the developing countries is harking back to models which had a history of failure, especially in Latin American and the Caribbean - President Truman's Puerto Rican "industrialization by invitation" model, ECLA's import substitution, President Kennedy's Alliance for Progress, President Johnson's regional integration, President Reagan's Caribbean Basin Initiative and President Bush's Enterprise for the Americas.

In contrast, East Asia, which is the fastest growing region without IMF/World Bank structural adjustment programs and handouts, has a capitalist market economy, but with the state playing a distinct interventionist role to prevent market distortions, to solve contradictions and to prevent marginalization.

A special report, **Our Own Agenda**, sponsored by the OAS and the IDB and prepared by the independent Latin America and Caribbean Commission on Development and Environment noted:

"Besides problems with direct environmental connotations, to which we have referred in part, other problems of an economic nature include:

• *The outflow of capital from Latin America and the Caribbean to the developed countries*

• *The constant deterioration of the prices of the raw materials produced by countries of the region*

• *The fluctuation of interest rates, fundamental in the worsening external debt problem*

• *The introduction of inappropriate technological patterns; and*

• *Commercial protectionism, among others*."

The net outflow of capital from Latin America and the Caribbean in the 1981-85 period was US$36 billion yearly in the form of profits, dividends and debt payments.

Developing countries lose US$500 billion annually through unequal international trade equivalent to 10 times the aid they receive from the developed countries.

Commodity price fluctuations, particularly for the one-crop and/or one mineral economies, had shattering effects. Every one per cent increase in interest rates in the North added nearly US$2.5 billion to the Latin American and Caribbean burdensome external indebtedness, which deprives the countries of the capital needed for growth, prolongs the grave economic crisis and exacerbates the condition of the poor.

Aid Fatigue; Donor Fatigue

Bilateral aid assistance is being cut, from 0.7 per cent of GNP to less than half that today. And the biggest countries are giving about a quarter.

Aid is being cut for the Caribbean countries. They cannot access soft loans. And it is being mooted that there are no prospects for the proposals put forward by my Government at the Summit of the Americas for a Regional Development Fund (RDF), Debt Relief and a Corps of Development Specialists for the creation of economic diversification and development - a level playing field - in anticipation of hemispheric free trade by the year 2005.

Meanwhile, the proposal of the British Government for sale of IMF gold reserves to provide debt relief for the highly-indebted countries has not been supported by the G7 nations.

Regrettably, at the same time, the top leaders of the

developed capitalist countries cannot present any prescriptions for curing the problems of the world economy. Symptoms, not the root causes, are treated. And the treatment is a palliative, a Band-Aid, like an aspirin to relieve the pain but not to cure it.

After the G7 "Jobs Summit" in Japan, a conference was held in Washington D.C. on poverty, and later another on unemployment in Detroit. The Development Committee of the World Bank and the IMF for the first time sponsored a meeting on "Population and Migration." But nothing tangible resulted.

"Jobs and Growth" was one of the most important themes of the G7 Naples Summit meeting. Its Economic Declaration noted: "*Unemployment remains far too high, with over 24 million unemployed in our countries alone. This is an unacceptable waste.*"

Modernized monopoly capitalism is unable to deal with recession, unemployment, financial deficit, trade frictions, the global environmental question, and the differences between the rich and the poor.

As the rich get richer at the expense of the poor in the developed North as well as the developing South, and the gap in living standards between the North and South continues to widen, there is generally a mood of gloom and concern about the future.

The president and founder, Klaus Schwab, and the managing director, Claude Smadja, of the prestigious World Economic Forum described this mood in a recent article "**Globalization Backlash is Serious**," in the *International Herald Tribune*. They wrote:

"*Economic globalization has entered a critical phase. A mounting backlash against its effects especially in the industrial democracies, is threatening to disrupt economic activity and social stability in many countries.*

The mood in these democracies is one of helplessness and anxiety. This can easily turn into revolt, as December's unrest in France showed."

Radical Reforms

In my address to the Annual Meeting of the Inter-American Development Bank in March 1993, I said: "*In Shakespeare's Julius Caesar, Cassius tells us: ' The fault, dear Brutus, is not in our stars, but in ourselves.' We need a correct theoretical perception of events, not only of the development of productive forces, but also of the relations of production and their contradictions. Piecemeal management is not enough. Nor can everything be left to be regulated only by the market. Both the market and the state, as the World Bank has noted, have irreplaceable, complementary roles.*"

In this period with the all-pervasive and predominant Western ideology, which has concluded "an end to history," very few dare, for fear of attacks, to put on the table a scientific, theoretical/ideological exposition of the root cause of the crisis. Today, any serious attempt to look at alternative strategies are looked upon with suspicion and some continue, to raise the communist red-herring. But those of us who have to answer to the masses of poor people must be able to find answers lest our people fall prey to those who would give them a false sense of security. Good governance, a democratic culture and accountability must be accompanied by concrete plans to solve real problems faced by real people.

Today, the obscurantists, the extreme religious/political Right, the xenophobes and the neo-fascists target the liberals, in the same way that attacks were leveled during the American War of Independence against Republicans (those wanting to break with the British Monarchy and the setting up of a Republic); against Tom Paine, the Englishman, who vigorously supported the independence struggle but was called "a dirty little atheist," and against the radicals and communists by the McCarthyite witch-hunters in the early 1950s.

With the collapse of communist rule in Eastern Europe and the Soviet Union, bipolar East/West political/ideological confrontation has abated. In its place has come the traditional intra-capitalist rivalry, which previously led to two world wars. Today, fierce competition has developed between the centers of world capitalism - North American, Europe and Japan.

The motive force of capitalist production of commodities is not use-value but the extraction of surplus value (profit, interest, rent, commissions). According to Tony Benn, British MP: "*Capitalism puts profit above people and modern capitalism, which has widened the gap between rich and poor even further, is not so much an economic system as a political system, frightening working people into obedience and enriching those who own and control the means of production, distribution and exchange."*

Modern, highly capital-intensive production methods with computers and robots entail huge capital expenditure on science, research and technology. Consequently, the greater share of the value of commodities accrue to capital rather than to labor.

As a result, increase in wages are not kept in step with the increase in productivity. This leads to higher levels of impoverishment and unemployment.

A development strategy for the eradication of poverty must be global and positive, not South against North and North against South, but the North and South in interdependence, cooperation and partnership. While our countries are individually searching for more positive and innovative ways to cope with this growing interdependence, globalization and liberalization that are taking place, there are emerging fundamental issues which can only be addressed by new global initiatives. Such initiatives were taken previously in times of crisis, like President Roosevelt's New Deal Programme, The Alliance for Progress, the Lome Convention, etc.

The liberal economist, Lord Maynard Keynes, proposed at the time of the Depression of the 1930s, state intervention and pump-priming of the economy.

In keeping with this tenet, President Roosevelt embarked on a radical reform program - a Works Program of physical, social and cultural infrastructure; a National Labor Relations Act (Wagner Act) and Board to fight against company unionism and goon squads; and the Sherman Act against monopolies. And his Governor in Puerto Rico, Rex Tugwell, carried out a radical land reform program and under the Fomento Plan constructed six factors - measures which are considered heretical today in the context of de-emphasizing and down-sizing the role of the state.

In my address to the United Nations, I stated that a New Global Human Order should be established on a sound and just system of global governance based on:

(1) A genuine North/South partnership and interdependence for

mutual benefit.

(2) A democratic culture that involved representation of, and consultation and participation with, the citizenry as a whole, supported by a lean and clean administration, transparent and accountable.

(3) A development strategy free from external domination and *diktat*. This strategy would emphasize sustainable, people-centered development with equity combined with a strong sensitivity towards issues of gender, the environment and the indigenous population.

(4) The application of science and technology for increased production and productivity. This is a *sine qua non* for any development and any program to eliminate poverty and backwardness.

(5) A global development facility funded by pollution taxes, cuts in military expenditure, a global tax on energy and a tax on speculative capital exchange movements. This could start easily with the savings from the elimination of weapons of mass destruction as an interim dividend to the long-awaited Peace Dividend.

Elaborating on this global development facility, I pointed out that it could be administered by a democratized and reformed United Nations for allocation, without undue conditions, to the developed and developing countries. A 3% cut in military spending, I noted could realize US$460 billion over a five year period, while a tax of US$1 on every barrel of oil produced (or its equivalent in coal) would realize around US$66 billion annually. A tax of 0.5% on global speculative capital movements, as suggested by Nobel Prize Winner, economist James Tobin, would yield US$1500 billion annually. There could also be a small airline ticket tax for long distance traveling. These funds could be used for a program of radical reforms which include:

(1) A massive works program for physical, social and cultural

infrastructure, modeled after the program of the Roosevelt New Deal Administration to overcome the ravages of the Great Depression of the 1930s. Another such plan was the Marshall Plan for the rebuilding of Europe after World War II.

(2) Increased employment by reducing the number of working days or the number of working hours per week, with no loss of pay. In addition the lowering of the retirement age, without loss of benefits.

(3) Tax and other incentives for the use of science and technology, which will accelerate the process of development and narrow the growing technological gap.

(4) A new European Union/African-Caribbean-Pacific Lome Convention with enhanced assistance for the developing countries.

(5) A refashioned Alliance for Progress for Latin America and the Caribbean.

(6) Debt relief for developing countries - debt cancellation; long term re-scheduling; a 10 per cent cap on debt payments in relation to export income.

(7) Major restructuring of the Multilateral Financial Institutions to respond to the challenges of a New Global Human Order.

Outside of radical reforms, the ruling circles of the developed and developing countries cannot escape the negative effects of the consequences of poverty and social disintegration. In an effort to promote peace, liberty and global prosperity through cooperation, and in order to meet the challenges ahead, human development must be comprehensive and allow for society's welfare to be assumed. Democracy can only prosper in an environment of economic, social and ecological development. Poverty atrophies the vigor and initiative of the individual and deprives the society of incalculable human resources. If left unattended, the expansion of poverty with hunger and the hopelessness it engenders will undermine the fabric of our civilization and the security of the democratic state, thus threatening world peace.

The ideological and political conflicts of the past between East and West must not be allowed to degenerate into a confrontation between "the haves" and "the have-nots" the "included" and the "excluded" and marginalized. There is need for the will among leaders in both the North and the South to establish relations of respect and recognition, that in our global village, the responsibility for its citizens lies not with a few but with all of us. Let us together, in the North and the South and in the East and West, strive for a New Global Human Order for peace, freedom and human development.

Georgetown Declaration on a New Global Human Order (1996)

In light of Dr. Jagan's exposition at the Conference on a New Global Human Order held from August 2-4, 1996 in Georgetown, Guyana, the Conference focussed its discussion on the following areas:

- Structural Adjustment, Liberalization and Globalization: Meaning and Consequences.

- The Challenge for Development and Alternative strategies.

- The Role of the State - Guyana

- A Case for Action - Agenda for a New Development Strategy and Partnership.

At the end of its deliberations the Conference agreed that:

- the present international order of economic globalization and liberalization does not function adequately in the interest of the peoples of the world. It fosters inequality between the North and the South as well as among the peoples in the South and in the North. It has frequently undermined long-term development prospects by reducing people's well-being, neglecting infrastructure and inhibiting investment;

- there is a need for a New Global Human Order that would ensure people-centered development based on the recognition of national sovereignty, participatory democracy, socio-economic equality and the realization of the social, economic and cultural rights enshrined in the United Nations Charter.

A New Program is necessary to give States a much wider

scope and responsibility for determining economic reforms required for the well-being of their peoples. To this end, immediate action must be taken to:

1. Find a solution to the debt crisis that involves the cancellation of the debt of the least developed countries (LDCs); significant reduction of multilateral debt; a reduction in the remaining debt stock to sustainable levels for other developing countries, with debt service payments limited to 10 per cent of exports, provided that 50 per cent of the savings is used for social-sector development;

2. increase significantly transfers of long-term development finance to developing countries by attaining the existing ODA target of 0.7 per cent of GNP through mobilizing new and additional sources of finance, creating a new Global Development Fund, and introducing measures to stabilize the international monetary system and financial markets;

3. establish a fair and equitable trading system, including the provision of reliable access to the markets of the North. Such a system should take account of the special needs of small developing states, ensure fair and stable commodity prices, and secure a renegotiation of the provisions of the World Trade Organization, especially with respect to trade and investment, intellectual property rights and services;

4. reduce and relax conditions attached to future financial transfers;

5. give new emphasis to the expansion of production and growth for sustainable development and a safe physical environment in the South;

6. develop the social sector as a focus of any new program, with emphasis on education, human

resources, health and the development needs of women, children and indigenous peoples;

7.   democratize and strengthen the United Nations and restructure other multilateral and financial institutions to respond more effectively to the challenge of people-centered development.

In order to carry forward this agenda:

1.   a Task Force should be established immediately to facilitate the review of current initiatives and help develop broad national, regional and international consensus for a New Global Human Order;

2.   a national, regional and international campaign should be mounted to increase awareness of the issues involved and to meet the challenges of the emerging New Global Human Order. In particular, steps should be taken to reach the broadest cross section of people through culture, the media, education, and other communication channels and techniques;

3.   constituencies of support should be built based on the maximum participation possible and a broad alliance of governments, NGOs, people's organizations, trade unions, religious organizations, indigenous peoples' organizations, academics, professionals, the private sector and others; and

4.   a Coordinating and Communication Center should be set up to facilitate the strengthening of the alliance.

Cheddi Jagan

Address to the World Food Summit in Rome, November 13-17, 1996

Presented by President Cheddi Jagan

Mr. Chairman, Distinguished Heads of State and Government, Secretary-General of the World Food Summit, Distinguished Delegates.

The 1974 World Food Conference proclaimed that "*every man, woman and child has the inalienable right to be free from hunger and malnutrition in order to develop their physical and mental faculties*." This was to have been achieved "within a decade," but we have failed, despite improvements in science and technology. Today, hunger, poverty and social disintegration stalk the globe, not just in the South but also in the North, and the gap in living standards between the North and the South continues to widen.

As we approach a new century, the South is faced with aid cuts and the North with "jobless recovery" and "jobless growth." Consequently, we need a new global partnership for sustainable human development, good governance and a development strategy, which will provide the world with sufficient food to have such food resources equitably distributed. Poverty is the root cause of food insecurity and only its rapid and permanent elimination will produce improved economic and social relations for a more equitable world order.

In an increasingly globalized environment of disorder and confusion, there is little room for concepts of development which place prime emphasis on the promotion of narrow national interests above the common good of humanity. A stop must be put to an unjust global economic order; an order which robs the South of about US$500 billion annually in unjust, non-equivalent international trade; an order where the poor South finances the North with South to North capital outflows of US$418 billion in the 1982-90 period as debt payments - a sum equal to six Marshall Plans which provided aid for the rehabilitation of Europe after World War II. Those payments did not even include outflows from royalties, dividends, repatriated profits and underpaid raw material.

In this decade, for the eradication of poverty, we need an Agenda for Development, with the right of nations to development, and, as His Holiness the Pope said, the right of the individual to food. Democracy must mean not just civil and political rights, but also economic, social and cultural rights. We must eliminate under-development, which threatens to undermine the very foundations of the global economy and society.

A new North/South partnership must be fashioned in the search for more positive and innovative ways to cope with the effects of globalization and liberalization, which are marginalizing millions of people and even many nations.

Many are of the opinion that these economic strategies constitute a panacea for development, but I stand here to say that the facts do not support such a view. The distinguished Gustave Speth, Head of the United Nations Development Program (UNDP), exposed the myth that privatization, free markets and foreign direct investment will obviate the need for development aid. If the real decline in aid to poor countries is allowed to continue, he says, the world will pay dearly through the tragic consequences of joblessness, environmental decay, conflict and violence.

During the 1980-1993 period, total official development assistance to agriculture fell by 55%. But there was also a reduction in the share of such assistance to such key areas as land and water development, research, rural development initiatives and agricultural extension. In this regard, I applaud the new emphasis by the World Bank on more development aid to the agricultural sector.

To stave off the danger of marginalization and to prevent being submerged by the rising tide of free trade, my Government at the 1994 Miami Summit, which approved a Free Trade Area of the Americas by the year 2005, proposed the establishment of a Regional Development (Integration) Fund, debt relief and a corps of development specialists/volunteers. Regrettably, the view is generally expressed that these realistic proposals would not materialize.

Poor Third World countries, such as Guyana, recognize the

symbiotic links between the environment, economic development, food security and human existence. We cannot therefore expect to eliminate starvation and food insecurity while so many countries continue to be ensnared in debt and thus lack the means to provide the basic services, which underpin economic development. For example, the attraction of foreign direct investment is dependent on civil peace, a basic productive infrastructure and a healthy and educated population. Yet my country has spent a total of US$308 million on foreign debt servicing over the last three years - an amount which was greater than all our capital inflows, a sum which was US$200 million greater than if debt payments did not exceed 10% of export income. As is the case in so many other debt-distressed countries, this situation has prevented my Government from channeling much-needed resources into such critical areas as poverty alleviation, rural development, agriculture, health, education and law enforcement. The Pope's call for a solution on moral and ethical grounds to Third World debt must be heeded.

My friends, we need a scientific, realistic and people-centered development strategy. This is why I have advocated the need for the development of a New Global Human Order, premised on sustainable economic development, equity, social and ecological justice, and based on the creation of a separate Global Development Fund for assistance to both the North and the South. We must put in place a system whose objectives will be to invest directly in the poor, to seek out opportunities for entrepreneurship among the marginalized, and to provide the social and infrastructural services which would enable the poor to become self-reliant and productive members of the global community. Specifically, I wish to advocate the following:

1. a limit on debt repayment equivalent to not more than 10% of export earnings;

2. the creation of regional integration funds to enable small economies to withstand the effects of globalization, liberalization and the formation of regional trading blocs. These funds would be used to invest in physical and social infrastructure, research

and development initiatives designed to yield productivity gains among the poor, and to improve the competitiveness of under-developed economies;

3. the time span for the realization of a Free Trade Area of the Americas to be the same as in the Asia-Pacific Economic Community (APC) - the year 2010 for the more developed countries and 2020 for the less developed countries;

4. a new and enhanced Lome Convention for the Third World;

5. a refashioned Alliance for Progress for Latin America and the Caribbean;

6. a democratic, lean and clean government; and

7. the earmarking of 20% of budgets by developing countries, and aid donors providing an equivalent 20% under the UNDP 20/20 Social Compact, for priority human development concerns.

Why should 40% of farm households in Guyana have five acres and less - with 58% of them being below the poverty line - in the context of a small population in a relatively large country with an abundance of water resources and arable land mainly in the state sector? Each farmer should and can have at least 100 acres, if not more, but the land must be drained and irrigated and protected from rising sea levels. Our farmers have demonstrated, during the past four years of my government, their capacity to increase agricultural production, but being so poor, they cannot be expected, under cost-recovery programs, to meet the huge expenditures on drainage and irrigation and sea and river defenses. Guyana needs debt relief, grants and soft loans, not only to become food self-sufficient but also to feed the food-deficient Latin American and Caribbean regions and the world.

This Summit affords us the opportunity to accelerate the process of addressing the situation of the poor and the powerless. As we leave Rome, we should be buoyed in the confidence that we have really charted the course towards greater food security. As I had cause to state at the G-7 Sectoral Meeting on Agriculture in Guyana early this year, if the rich and poor countries do not act together to overcome the problems of poverty, and the attendant maladies of hunger and environmental degradation, there will be no secure peace.

If, therefore, there is cause to meet again in another twenty years, it should be to celebrate the achievements of this Summit and the full implementation of its Plan of Action.

Cheddi Jagan

Free and Fair Trade is a Prerequisite for Integration

In what was his last official public speaking engagement, Dr. Cheddi Jagan, on February 13,1997, addressed the Sixth Meeting of the Free Trade Area of the Americas Working Group on Smaller Economies.

Following is the full text of the address delivered at the Pegasus Hotel, Georgetown, Guyana.

On behalf of the Government and people of Guyana, I extend to you a warm welcome to our country, and wish you every success in your deliberations during this Sixth Meeting of the FTAA Working Group on Smaller Economies.

I do hope that, in spite of your busy schedule you will take the opportunity to have a glimpse of our small but beautiful country and enjoy the traditional Guyanese hospitality.

Permit me to pay tribute to the outstanding work which has been accomplished so far by the Working Group on Smaller Economies. We are indebted to Ambassador Richard Bernal of Jamaica for his dedicated, astute and efficient chairmanship.

I am convinced that with continued hard work by this Group, the growth and development of the Smaller Economies can only redound to the benefit of the entire hemisphere .

Mr. Chairman, Distinguished Delegates, like the other Small Economies in the hemisphere, Guyana is grappling with the cosmic trends of globalization and trade liberalization. At the same time we are making every effort to adjust in a rapidly changing economic and political process to avoid marginalization.

As I see it, given current global trends, there is no alternative but to combine our human and other resources as we seek to achieve a friction-free harmonious and collectively beneficial Free Trade Area, that will be characterized by the removal of tariff and non-tariff barriers. As I have said on more than one occasion, as regards the Smaller Economies, we either swim together or sink together in the rising tide of free trade and the sea levels.

Mr. Chairman, I am on record at various fora, as having

expressed serious concern about the plights of Smaller Economies, not only in our Hemisphere, but in the entire global system. Many of our countries are experiencing onerous debt problems, grinding poverty, high unemployment and increasing social disintegration. Our countries are seeking debt relief from commercial creditors and other multilateral financial institutions in order to advance the development process for the benefit of our peoples.

A definite solution must be found for the Third World's crushing external debt problem. It has now reached unmanageable levels. Its net present value is more than 200 per cent of annual exports. In Latin America and the Caribbean, with 181 million out of 441 million people living below the poverty line in the mire of destitution, how can human development take place when, despite onerous debt payments, the stock of debt grows. Between 1981 and 1990 the region's foreign debt payments were US$503 billion, of which interest was US$313 billion. "*At the same time, the region's consolidated external debt rose from US$297 billion in 1981 to US$428 billion in 1990. The mechanism whereby the more you pay the more you owe is perverse and must be stopped*," noted the 1992 UNICEF publication **Children of the Americas**.

The present mechanism whereby "*the more you pay, the more you owe*" is in need of urgent review. It is some consolation that the IMF and World Bank leaders are now recognizing the need for urgent solutions to these problems. The IMF seems willing now to sell part of its gold reserves to assist poorer countries with their debt problems, an idea which was mooted many years ago but is still being opposed by some members of the G7 nations. Debt relief in the form of debt cancellation, grants, soft loans and rescheduling is urgent, if the developing countries are to eradicate poverty, protect the environment, play their meaningful role in expanding world trade and help end stagnation and recession in the industrially-developed countries. Debt relief must be seen as an investment not only in the development of poor countries but also in the security of the rich nations.

Because of the debt trap, we are unable to urgently address and find solutions to help alleviate the suffering of the working people and to provide them with the basic needs for their survival. I have never been associated with "Prophets of Doom." Rather, I have always been and will always be a supreme optimist. I must say, however, that given recent and current social and political upheavals in several countries in our hemisphere, I am convinced that time is running out. We have to move quickly to solve the mounting social and economic problems occurring in our countries.

At the Summit of the Americas Meeting in Miami in December 1994, I reiterated the urgent need for a New Global Human Order within the framework of a *"New Agenda for Development."* I expressed the view that while we embrace the practice of good governance and participatory democracy in the hemisphere, there is also a need to give full attention to the gaps between the rich and the poor, the techno-skilled and the techno-unskilled, and between the North and the South.

In this regard, given existing social and economic realities in our hemisphere, as manifested in the wide disparities between and among us, it is only logical that there should be special and preferential treatment for the less fortunate, in order to facilitate their active and productive participation in the integration process and to increase their levels of development. Free and fair trade is a basic prerequisite for any successful integration of the Americas.

As we move inexorably towards the establishment of a hemispheric free trade area, it is becoming increasingly evident that a special facility should be created to help the weaker economies play a real partnership role in such a collective endeavor. My rationale for calling for the establishment of such a facility is to be found in the fact that there are in our hemisphere larger economies which obviously stand to benefit more than those that can be described as Smaller Economies.

The fact that a few states in our hemisphere, developed and developing, are producing similar products utilizing processes and technology, which are decades apart, is a reality that should be taken into consideration. This does not augur well for fair competition and, moreover, confirms to the dictum that there should be equality among equals and proportionality among unequals.

In this regard, we should take a leaf from the European and South-East Asian experiences. In the EEC mega-bloc, the leaders were more perceptive and understood the inherent problems in liberalizing trade between countries of varying levels of economic and social development. The integration of Europe provides for the free movement, not only of capital, services and goods, but also of people. For the lesser developed countries, like Greece, Spain, Portugal and Ireland, a special Development Fund has been established to raise per capita income to at least the level of seventy-five percent of the Community's average income. Under NAFTA, there is no such provision even though the disparities in development and income levels are far wider in the Western Hemisphere than in Western Europe.

In the Far East APE integration movement, agreed to at the same time as NAFTA, a realistic differential time-frame for the attainment of free trade has been instituted, 10 years for the more developed countries and 20 years for the lesser developed countries.

Mr. Chairman, Distinguished Delegates, you are aware that Guyana has been promoting the concept of the Regional Development Fund, now called the Regional Integration Fund. In June 1995, consultations were held in Georgetown and recommendations were unanimously adopted, calling for further consultations on the proposal with the Working Group on Smaller Economies itself, the Caribbean Community and other hemispheric organizations.

The response to this initiative is most encouraging. Studies done by the Organization of American States, the Inter-American Development Bank, the Latin American Economic System, the Economic Commission for Latin American and the Caribbean, and the Caribbean Development Bank were basically supportive of special measures to assist the Smaller Economies within the context of the Free Trade Area of the Americas. In many respects, many of the conclusions arrived at in these studies coincided with the thrust of the proposal for a Regional Integration Fund.

As part of the preparations for the Fifth Meeting of this Working Group, which took place in Caracas, Guyana hosted a second round of consultations on the Regional Integration Fund proposal. These consultations benefited from the full support of the Caribbean Community Secretariat, SELA and ECLAC and several countries of this hemisphere. Indeed, Bolivia and Honduras have formulated proposals which are not dissimilar from the RIF proposal.

Subsequent to the Caracas Meeting, the Government of Guyana in collaboration with the Caribbean Community Secretariat, prepared a consolidated working paper on the subject which I understand, is a key Working Document of this Sixth Session of the Working Group on Smaller Economies.

As witnessed by the Second Hemispheric Trade Ministerial Meeting, which was held in Cartagena, Colombia, in March 1996, and the Caribbean Community/Central America Foreign Ministers Meeting which was held in San Jose, Costa Rica in December last year, it is also my understanding that there is an emerging hemispheric consensus on the necessity for the establishment of the Fund.

I hope too that a consensus will emerge on the burdensome foreign debt, which inhibits the development of our countries. They should not have to make debt payments exceeding ten per cent of export income. Also, that the APEC time frame should be adopted for the FTAA.

The Government of Canada has expressed its willingness to discuss the RIF as a Caricom Initiative with other interested parties. I look forward to the Government of the United States giving the Proposal the support it deserves.

Mr. Chairman, I am convinced that arising from your deliberations in Georgetown, concrete and positive recommendations will emerge as regards the objectives, financing and management of the Fund.

This will ensure that, as we move from the Second Trade Vice-Ministers' Meeting later this month in Brazil, to the Third Trade Ministerial Meeting in May, also to be held in Brazil, there would be tangible progress with regard to support for the establishment of a Regional Integration Fund, and consequently placing the proposal firmly in the mainstream of the process leading up to the realization of the FTAA.

Let me add that of immediate need to our Smaller Economies is the provision of technical assistance to facilitate, during this preparatory process, our countries' greater participation in the FTAA and the eleven specialized Working Groups and the actual negotiating process.

Mr. Chairman, Distinguished Delegates, Ministers of Government, Ladies and Gentlemen, it pleases me to know that Guyana is playing host to this Sixth Meeting of the FTAA Working Group on Smaller Economies.

It gives me great satisfaction to know that Guyana is making a modest contribution to laying the basis for free and fair trade practices in this hemisphere.

I am also proud of the fact that Guyana is making a modest contribution to the process leading up to the negotiations of the FTAA. I am convinced that, as long as we view this process, not only as a partnership, but as the forging of our collective destiny aimed at serving the interests of our people, we can together, create in this hemisphere the world's most important and vibrant free trade area.

I thank you.

Books by Cheddi Jagan

Forbidden Freedom -1954, 1955, 1989, 1994, 1997
The West on Trial - 1966, 1967, 1972, 1975, 1980, 1997
The Caribbean Revolution -1979
The Caribbean: Whose Backyard? -1984
Selected Speeches 1992-1994 - 1995
My Fight for Guyana's Freedom - 1998
The USA in South America -1998

Booklets, Pamphlets and Papers

Bitter Sugar - 1949
Fight For Freedom - Waddington Constitution Exposed - 1952
Is Imperialism Dead? - 1953
Towards Independence - 1958
Towards Understanding - Address to National Press Club - Oct. 1961
Speech by Dr. Cheddi Jagan before the Economic Commission for Latin America and Chile - 1961
British Guiana's Future - Peaceful or Violent - 1963
My Credo - Circa 1963
The Anatomy of Poverty in British Guiana - 1964
US Intervention in Guyana - 1966
The Role of the CIA in Guyana and its activities throughout the world - 1967
The Coalition Exposed - 1967
Guyana: a Bed of Thorns - Cheddi Jagan and Clement Rohee - 1968
Socialism For Guyana - 1968
Caribbean Unity and Carifta - 1968
Border Conspiracy Exposed - Text of Legislation Speech on Venezuela Decree - 1968
The Role of the Opposition in the Caribbean
The Truth about Bauxite Nationalization - 1971
A West Indian State: Pro-lmperialist or Anti-lmperialist - 1972
Race and Politics in Guyana - Cheddi Jagan and Ram Karran - 1974
The Caribbean and the Centers of International Power - 1974
The Struggle For a Socialist Guyana - 1975
The Superiority of Scientific Socialism - Cheddi Jagan and Clinton Collymore -1975

Cheddi Jagan on Critical Support - 1976
Trade Unions and National Liberation - 1977
Poverty - Cause and Cure in the Developing Countries - 1978
The State of the Free Press in Guyana - Cheddi Jagan and
    Moses Nagamootoo - 1980
The IMF Takes Over - 1982
Strengthen the Party! Defend the Masses! Liberate Guyana!
Text of Central Committee Report to PPP Congress - 1982
Non-Alignment as a viable Alternative For Regional
    Cooperation - 1982
Non-Alignment: Force for Peace and Social Progress- 1983
Unmasking the Enemies of the Guyanese People - 1984
The Caribbean - A Zone of Peace - 1985
PPP Struggles for TUC Freedom 1985
For a Revolutionary Democratic Alliance - Speeches by
    C.Jagan, G. Daniels and J. Pollydore - 1985
Yes to Marxism - Cheddi Jagan and Walter Rodney - 1985
The PPP and the Private Sector - Cheddi Jagan and Clinton
    Collymore - 1986
Cheddi Jagan speaks to Workers on May Day 1986
Unity and Action in the Youth Movement - Cheddi Jagan and
    Earl Bousquet - 1986
The 1987 Budget: A Sell-out to the IMF - 1987
Tracing Our Paths in a Changing World - 1990
Our Footsteps and our Vision for a Free Guyana - 1991
Race, Class and Nationhood - Cheddi Jagan and Moses
    Nagamootoo - 1993
Global Dilemma: Economic Growth, Debt Burden -1994
The National Democratic State -1994
New Global Human Order - The Fight Against Poverty -
    1994-1996